AN ANTONINE FORT
GOLDEN HILL, DUNTOCHER

For Mrs. Hilda Miller
in memory of her husband,
S.H. Miller, whose teaching
and example had such a
strong influence on the
grateful writer of this book,
his pupil,
Anne S. Robertson.

AN ANTONINE FORT
Golden Hill, Duntocher

AN ACCOUNT OF EXCAVATIONS CARRIED
OUT ON THE ANTONINE WALL AND FORT
ON GOLDEN HILL, DUNTOCHER
DUNBARTONSHIRE

UNDER THE AUSPICES OF
THE UNIVERSITY OF GLASGOW

BY

ANNE S. ROBERTSON
Dalrymple Lecturer in Archæology
and Under-Keeper of the Hunterian Museum

Published for the University of Glasgow

BY

OLIVER AND BOYD
EDINBURGH : TWEEDDALE COURT
LONDON : 39A WELBECK STREET, W. 1

FIRST PUBLISHED 1957

Grateful acknowledgment is made of generous financial assistance from the Carnegie Trust for the Universities of Scotland towards the cost of publication.

PRINTED IN GREAT BRITAIN BY
OLIVER AND BOYD LTD., EDINBURGH

CONTENTS

GOLDEN HILL, DUNTOCHER

SUMMARY AND CONCLUSIONS

ILLUSTRATIONS

TEXT FIGURES

FIGURES AT END OF VOLUME

PLATES AT END OF VOLUME

ABBREVIATIONS

Arch. Ael.	Archæologia Aeliana
Arch. Journ.	Archæological Journal
Balmuildy	S. N. Miller, *The Roman Fort at Balmuildy* (1922)
Bar Hill	Macdonald and Park, *The Roman Forts on the Bar Hill* (1906)
Cadder	John Clarke, *The Roman Fort at Cadder* (1933)
Castledykes	*The Roman Occupation of South-Western Scotland* (1952), pp. 127 ff.
C.I.L.	Corpus Inscriptionum Latinarum
Déchelette	J. Déchelette, *Les Vases Céramiques ornés de la Gaule romaine* (1904)
Dragendorff	H. Dragendorff, *Terra Sigillata*, in Bonner Jahrbucher, XCVI-XCVII (1895-96)
J.R.S.	Journal of Roman Studies
N.S.A.	New Statistical Account of Scotland
Old Kilpatrick	S. N. Miller, *The Roman Fort at Old Kilpatrick* (1928)
Oswald	F. Oswald, *Index of Figure Types on Terra Sigillata*, I (1937)
P.S.A.S.	Proceedings of the Society of Antiquaries of Scotland
R.W.	Sir George Macdonald, *The Roman Wall in Scotland* (1934)
Trans. Cumb. and West A.S.	Transactions of the Cumberland and Westmorland Antiquarian and Archæological Society
Yorks. Arch. Journ.	Yorkshire Archæological Journal

GOLDEN HILL, DUNTOCHER

GOLDEN HILL, Duntocher, lies 9 miles north-west of Glasgow and about 200 feet above sea-level. Its subsoil is boulder clay, overlying the calciferous sandstone series (Nat. Grid. Ref. NS 495726).

The hill is a plateau with a very gentle incline to north-east, east and south-east, a less gentle slope to the south, and an abrupt drop to the west and north-west. At the foot of the steep west and north-western slope runs the Duntocher Burn.

Golden Hill commands a wide view in almost all directions, except to the north-west and north, where frown the Kilpatrick Hills. To the north-east is the Blane Valley gap. To the east there stands in clear view, 2 miles away, Castlehill, near Bearsden, long recognised as the site of an Antonine Wall fort. To the south-west and south there must, in Roman times, have been an uninterrupted outlook across the River Clyde, over ground now occupied by the shipyards, engineering works and houses of Clydebank and Dalmuir. To the west, as noted in Gough's Camden,[1] the hill " commands a view of the River Clyde till stopped by the hills of Cowell in Argyleshire, near 20 miles distant " (Plates 3, 5).

Across this hill there ran the Antonine Wall and Ditch, in their course from Forth to Clyde, and on part of the hill there stood an Antonine Wall fort (see map, Fig. 20).

THE HISTORY OF THE SITE

In the second edition of his *Roman Wall in Scotland* (1934) Sir George Macdonald gave the following description of the line taken by the Antonine Wall and Ditch over Golden Hill [2] :

Rather more than three-quarters of a mile beyond the stepping-stones over the burn (i.e. the Cleddans Burn), when close to a clump

---

[1] Gough's Camden (1806), IV, p. 102.   [2] *R.W.*, pp. 176 f.

of beech-trees, the line takes a further turn towards the right, and
makes straight for the site of the next station, the fort of Duntocher on
the summit of the Golden Hill, 700 or 800 yards to the north-west.
After traversing the corner of a golf course, it is momentarily lost beneath
a wider and more frequented road, which meets it at right angles. But
it is easily found again on the farther side, as it enters upon a long and
steady ascent. In certain conditions of the crop, the impress left by
the Ditch can be followed from a solitary tree near the foot of the
field all the way to the crest. At the low wall, which it encounters
there, the middle of the barely distinguishable hollow is some 60 yards
distant from the hedge on the south.

Within the next field Rampart and Ditch are presently called upon
to serve as the northern defences of the *castellum*, the position of which
is marked by a series of low mounds, too indefinite for accurate planning.
Once these have been passed there is a rapid descent, with no appreci-
able change of direction, to the Duntocher (or Dalmuir) Burn, the bank
of which is reached close to the so-called " Roman Bridge." The
remains of the Ditch are quite perceptible upon the slope, and it is
virtually certain that the stone foundation of the Rampart is still intact
beneath the turf. The gradient here is so formidable as to warrant
us in assuming that there may have been a by-pass for the Road at
some distance to the south and west. If so, there is no record of any
trace of it having been observed. On the other hand, during at least
the first half of the eighteenth century, as the contemporary plans and
descriptions show, the Military Way proper could be plainly seen
approaching the east gate and then turning to the left in order to pass
along the south front, just as it did at Cadder. At the south-west corner
it turned to the right again and began to make its way downhill. It
was in uncommonly fine condition—" very grand in the third degree
at least," as Horsley puts it.[1] That its appearance had made a deep
impression on a much older generation is proved by the place-name.
" Duntocher " is a Celtic word and means " the causeway-fort." [2]

In a later passage,[3] Sir George discussed the evidence to
be gleaned from earlier antiquaries regarding the Antonine
Wall fort on Golden Hill. The accounts of these antiquaries
are confused and conflicting, and although agreeing that
there was an Antonine Wall fort on the hill, they fail to
establish with certainty its exact position and dimensions.

[1] *Britannia Romana* (1732), p. 164.
[2] Watson, *Celtic Place-names of Scotland* (1926), p. 486.
[3] *R.W.*, pp. 328 ff.

Alexander Gordon, for example, notes that

upon the East Bank of which (i.e. the Duntocher Burn), the Ground rising considerably, are to be seen the distinct Vestiges of another Roman Fort, the Form and Dimensions of which, as it appears and measures to this Day, I give you in Pl. xvi.[1]

Pl. xvi shows the fort as a square with rounded corners, of unspecified dimensions, with the Military Way skirting the southern defences, one gate in the south side and the Antonine Wall itself bisecting the fort so that part of it projected beyond the Wall.

John Horsley, a most careful observer, gives the following description of the fort [2] :

The fort of Duntocher is situated at the top of the rising ground, that ascends from the water ; and by reason of its high situation has a large prospect. The north rampart, or that part of the wall which forms it, runs along the very top of the hill ; and the fort stands upon a gentle declivity open to the south ; a situation I have frequently observed to be much liked and chosen by the Romans. A small branch of the military way enters the east gate of the fort, but the grand way goes round it. The figure and dimensions of the fort appear from the draught of it. Some curious Roman antiquities, stones and medals, have been found here.

In Horsley's plan, the fort is represented as approximately square in shape, abutting on the Antonine Wall, having no gate in the north side, but with gates in the west, east and south sides. The Military Way skirted the southern defences, sending off a branch to the east gate, and a shorter branch to the south gate.

By the time General William Roy visited the site, in 1753, the remains of the fort were less clearly visible.

Little more of this station exists than what is barely sufficient to trace its dimensions. Towards the west end some vestiges of a præ-torium, or other building, may be perceived ; and the military way, having from the river ascended the hill in a sweep, passes on the south side of the fort.[3]

Roy's plan indicates that the fort had only one gate, in the

---

[1] *Itinerarium Septentrionale* (1726), p. 51.
[2] *Britannia Romana* (1732), pp. 164 f.
[3] *Military Antiquities* (1793), p. 158 and Pl. xxxv.

south side, and measured about 430 feet from east to west by about 290 from north to south. This would give it an internal area of about 2¾ acres.

In 1775, there came to light on Golden Hill the ruins of a Roman building, the recorded description of which shows it to have been a bath-house. Its discovery was first mentioned by John Knox, of Old Kilpatrick, in a book which bears the delightful title *A View of the British Empire, more especially Scotland* (1785), p. 611 n. :

Near the western extremity of this wall, at Duntocher, a countryman, in digging a trench upon the declivity of a hill, turned up several uncommon tiles, which exciting the curiosity of the peasantry in that neighbourhood, they broke in upon an entire subterraneous building, from which they dug out a cart load of excellent tiles. Being then, 1775, upon my return from the Highlands, and hearing of the circumstance, I repaired immediately to the place, and by threats and promises put a stop to all further proceedings, in the hope that some public spirited gentlemen would take off the surface, and explore the whole plan of the building, without demolishing it. The tiles were of 7 different sizes, the smallest being 7, and the largest 21 inches square. They were from 2 to 3 inches in thickness, of a reddish colour, and in perfect sound condition. The lesser ones composed several rows of pillars, which formed a labyrinth of passages, of about 18 inches high, and the same in width ; the largest tiles being laid over these pillars, served as a roof to support the earth on the surface, which was two feet deep, and had been plowed through time immemorial. The building was surrounded by a subterraneous wall of hewn stone. Some professors in the university of Glasgow, and other gentlemen, having unroofed the whole, discovered the appearances of a Roman hot-bath. The passages formed by rows of pillars were strowed with the bones and teeth of animals, and a sooty kind of earth ; in the bath was placed the figure of a woman cut in stone, which, with a set of the tiles, and other curiosities found in this place, is deposited in the university.

On the summit of the hill stood the Roman fort or castella (*sic*), of which Mr Gordon hath given a drawing. The foundation was lately erased by a clerk, or overseer of an iron manufactory in that neighbourhood, who was, however, disappointed in his expectations of finding treasure. The same Goth expressed a strong desire to erase a fine remain of the Roman wall, which is carried along the base of the hill, but he hath not succeeded in his wishes, and it rests with the family of Blantyre, to prevent such practices in future, upon grounds of which they are the superiors.

The *Old Statistical Account of Scotland*, v (1793), p. 238, copies Knox's account of the discovery of the baths, and Gough's Camden (1806), IV, p. 102, gives additional details, and sketches, " obtained from a correspondent on the spot." These place the bath-house to the north-west of the fort, not far from the site of the present church.

Robert Stuart reviews the accounts given by earlier antiquaries of the fort and bath-house, but assumes that two different discoveries of a subterranean building were made in 1775.[1] As Sir George Macdonald noted,[2] this was due to his following two different versions of the same discovery. The *New Statistical Account of Scotland*, VIII (1845), p. 22, refers briefly to the building, adding that " now, there is nothing to mark the excavation, but a small sinking in the surface above where the cavity was situated."

Movable Roman finds from Golden Hill seem mostly to have been associated with the bath-house. The " figure of a woman cut in stone," mentioned by Knox, is apparently a nymph, holding a large shell pierced with an opening for water. It is now in the Hunterian Museum.[3] The " set of the tiles, and other curiosities found in the place " are not, however, now to be found in the Museum. Nor are the " bones and teeth of animals " of Knox's account.

From the bath-house too, came the fragments of two Samian bowls (form 37) and of two mortaria rims, one stamped BRVSC F, which are described and illustrated in Gough's Camden.[4] They are of Antonine date. Other potsherds, some of them of Samian ware, " a piece of lead as if cut from a bar or pig " and two pieces of window glass were also found,[5] besides " some husks of grain." [6] Other finds recorded from the vicinity of the fort are " a Roman altar without any inscription . . . found in a field in the neighbourhood," " Roman querns . . . found in the adjacent places," and " a Roman vase . . . found in one

---

[1] *Caledonia Romana*, 2nd ed. (1852), pp. 295 ff.   [2] *R.W.*, p. 331.
[3] *R.W.*, pp. 444 f. and Pl. LXXVII, 5.   [4] P. 102, and Pl. VI.
[5] Gough's Camden (1806), IV, p. 102.   [6] *N.S.A.* VIII (1845), p. 22.

of the fields of Auchintoshan estate, the property of John Cross Buchanan, Esq." [1] The present location of these finds is not known.

Finally, at least eight Roman coins have been recorded from Duntocher. They are as follows [2] :

	AV	AR	AE
Vespasian	1		
Domitian		1	
Trajan		1	1
Hadrian	1		
Antoninus Pius			2
Faustina 1		1	
	2	3	3

Any, or all, of these coins might have been lost during the Antonine period.

At the time of the publication of the second edition of *The Roman Wall in Scotland* (1934), then, the site of the Antonine Wall fort at Duntocher was known to lie somewhere on Golden Hill. The only indication of its dimensions was the plan made by Roy (which in fact is now known to be erroneous), and accepted by later writers. A few trial trenches cut by Mr John Clarke in 1933 did not succeed in discovering any recognisable remains of the fort defences. And not a trace of these defences can now be seen either on the ground or from the air. Nevertheless, an area of Golden Hill which was thought to cover the site of the fort was scheduled by the Ministry of Works. Most of this area lies within a public park owned by Old Kilpatrick District Council.

THE PRELIMINARY EXCAVATION OF 1947

It was in October 1947 that the University of Glasgow, through the Hunterian Museum, was offered the opportunity of once again conducting excavations on Golden Hill, the site of the earliest recorded excavations by members of its staff. The part of the hill concerned, however, was not the western but the eastern slope.

[1] *Ibidem.*   [2] *P.S.A.S.*, LII (1918), p. 226, and LXXXIV (1950), p. 158.

On this slope of Golden Hill, between the road from Clydebank to Hardgate, and the site of Golden Hill Public Park, the ground was being prepared, in 1947, for the construction of a new housing scheme. The County Council of Dunbartonshire, which was responsible for the housing scheme, agreed to a request by the Inspectorate of Ancient Monuments of the Ministry of Works that several trenches should be cut under my supervision across the presumed line of the Antonine Wall and Ditch in the area concerned, in order that their exact position and dimensions might be ascertained before they were hidden from view.

The line of the Wall and Ditch was traced for about 700 feet (Fig. 1). The Ditch was 20-21 feet broad and about 8 feet deep, and had the now familiar V-shaped outline (Fig. 2). The stone foundation of the Antonine Wall lay at a distance of 30 feet to the south of the Ditch and had the unusually generous breadth of 16 feet. Although less than a foot under the surface, it was in extremely good preservation. The stones had been laid and levelled with care. The turf superstructure of the Wall, on the other hand, had been almost completely ploughed away. The only surviving traces of it were scraps of decayed turf embedded in interstices of the stone foundation.

As a result of this emergency excavation, the Hunterian Museum made plans for a larger-scale excavation on Golden Hill, with the aim of tracing the line of the Antonine Wall and Ditch westwards over the hill, and of locating the exact site of the fort and learning something of its dimensions and plan. This programme was made possible in the first instance by the approval of the Ancient Monuments Board of the Ministry of Works, and in the second instance by the consent and co-operation of several different landowners and their tenants. These were Mr W. Dunn Black, the owner of land on the eastern slope of the hill, and his tenant, Mr P. Moreland, of Braidfield Farm, Duntocher ; Mr A. D. Black, Miss E. A. Black and Miss J. E. C. Black, joint owners of the adjoining field to the west ; and

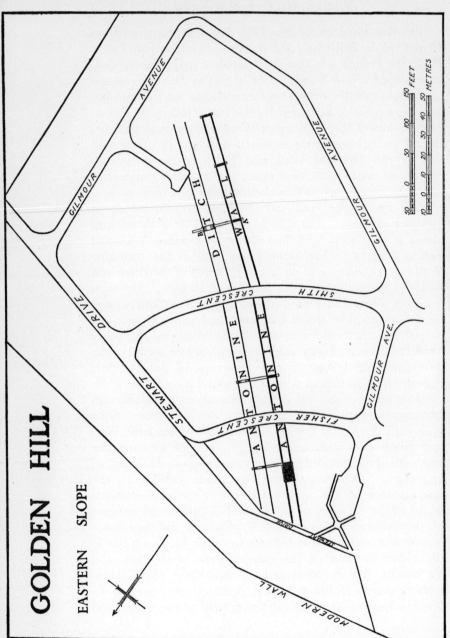

Fig. 1. Line of Antonine Wall and Ditch on eastern slope of Golden Hill. (Based on a Ministry of Works plan)

Old Kilpatrick District Council, tenants of the last-named field, which was then in use for allotments, and owners of Golden Hill Public Park, which adjoined the allotments on their west side.

Excavation began in September 1948, and continued for seven weeks. This was followed by two further periods of excavation, lasting respectively for five weeks and seven weeks, in the spring and autumn of 1949, and by a final week's work in the spring of 1951. The cost of the excavations was borne entirely by the Hunterian Museum, Glasgow University, at the suggestion of Professor J. D. Mackie, Honorary Curator of the Cultural Collections in the Museum, and the work was greatly facilitated throughout by the assistance of Mr George Hutchison, and Mr William Hood, then on the staff of the Museum, and of Mr W. Ballantyne, B.SC., and Mr J. Galloway, B.SC., then on the staff of the Civil Engineering Department of the University.

The labour force of paid workmen was supplemented by a number of University students who spent varying periods of time on the site. Most of these were students of Glasgow University. Of the others, one came from Edinburgh University, one from Oxford, one from Durham, and two from American Universities. All made a useful contribution to the work, and out of so many special mention can only be made of those who spent the longest time on the site, Mr Frank Newall, M.A., who has since undertaken independent excavations of his own at the recently discovered Roman site at Whitemoss Farm, Bishopton, Renfrewshire, Mr H. Sinclair, and Mr J. H. H. Baxter, M.A.

Mr John Clarke, M.A., and the late Mr S. N. Miller, M.A., discussed the excavations with me, and Mr Clarke read the report in typescript. Dr J. A. Smythe, King's College, Newcastle, contributed an appendix on a piece of piping which proved to be of modern origin, and Dr J. F. Hyslop, through Mr Charles Taylor, made analyses of three pieces of brick whose Roman character was suspect.

To Mrs A. Hallifax Crawford, too, grateful thanks

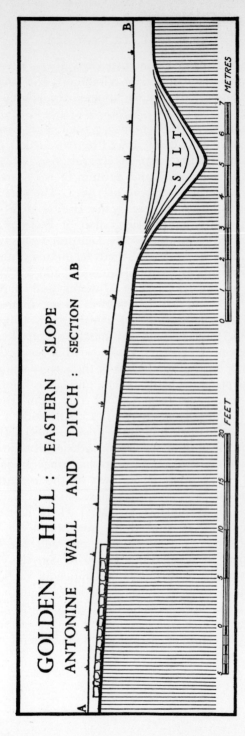

Fig. 2. Section AB across Antonine Wall and Ditch on eastern slope of Golden Hill. (Based on a Ministry of Works section)

are due for her untiring patience in cleaning up stonework, and for many other friendly acts on the site. Finally, acknowledgment must be made of the hospitality so generously extended by Mrs P. McGarry, Stewart Drive, Hardgate. This was particularly appreciated in the autumn of 1948, when almost continuous rain on a site with a clay subsoil turned excavation into a waterlogged nightmare.

The Excavations of 1948-51

In 1948, the Antonine Wall and Ditch were traced westwards from the site of the housing scheme. It was found that for a distance of about 370 feet, in addition to the length of about 700 feet traced in the housing area, that is, for about 360 yards in all, the Wall base maintained a width of 16 feet, the Ditch a width of 20 feet, and the interval between them a span of about 30 feet.

In several sections the Ditch was found to have had large stones set on its outer or north edge. At one point, a well-preserved stone culvert was discovered running across the stone foundation of the Antonine Wall (Fig. 21 and Plate 1). It was close on 1 foot wide, and 8 inches deep. Its sides were formed of large stones, roughly squared on the inner face, it was floored by stone flags and covered by large flat stones, averaging about 18 inches in width. Most of the cover slabs were still in position.

The purpose of the culvert was apparently to drain off water from the south side of the Antonine Wall, and moisture from its turf superstructure, into the Antonine Ditch, although the slope from south to north was very slight. Such culverts appear to have been provided at frequent intervals along the line of the Wall. Other well-preserved examples have been recorded from the line of the Wall near Mumrills,[1] near Bar Hill [2] and at Hillfoot.[3]

Persistent trenching in the same year, 1948, on the south side of the Antonine Wall, in the area to the west of

[1] *R.W.*, p. 84 and Pl. x, 2.   [2] *R.W.*, p. 84 and Pl. x, 1.
[3] *R.W.*, p. 165 and Pl. xxvi.

the site of the culvert, brought to light many scraps of
Roman pottery and tile fragments,[1] affording proof of
Roman occupation nearby, and at last revealed the position
of the fort itself. With the discovery of the fort came the
first of a series of surprises. The fort was tiny, far far smaller
than General Roy's plan suggests.[2] Its internal area was
only about half an acre. It was enclosed by a turf rampart
set on a stone base, and it lay on the southern slope of the
hill with two or three hundred feet of level dead ground
to the north (Fig. 3).[3]

In the spring of 1949 the apparently unsuitable and
indeed unlikely position of the fort was confirmed by further
trenching, and an examination of the level expanse to the
north was rewarded by the discovery that the Antonine
Ditch had been accompanied by an outer ditch, running
parallel to it and at a distance of about 36 feet from it. Three
ditches were found on the east and south sides of the fort.
Further, the fort was found to have had gates in the north,
east and west sides, but none in the south side, the only
side in which the earlier antiquaries had agreed in placing
a gate.[4] Then, outside the west gate of the fort there was
identified a structure which appeared to have been a small
military enclosure attached to the fort and enclosed by a
turf rampart set on a stone base. Its most puzzling characteristic was the impression it gave of having been in existence
before the fort, whose north rampart seemed to have been
built up against it.

---

[1] The tile fragments were one piece of flue tile, scored with a diamond
pattern, one piece of flanged roof tile, one piece of a semicylindrical roofing
tile and four nondescript tile fragments. See below, p. 74, Nos. 3, 5, 6, 11-14.

The potsherds comprised an amphora fragment, a mortarium fragment,
a piece of the rim and side of a beaker, two more beaker fragments, a piece of a
heavy platter, pieces of a finer platter, nine fragments of a fine bowl made in
imitation of a Samian bowl, two fragments of lids and an indeterminate scrap.
See below, p. 79, No. 10c ; p. 83, Nos. 21, 22a, 22b, 24, 25 ; p. 85, No. 30 ;
p. 86, Nos. 44, 45 ; p. 87, No. 50.

[2] See above, p. 4.

[3] The fort actually faces north-east. In the following pages, for the sake
of convenience, the front of the fort is described as the north front, and the
other three sides accordingly.   [4] See above, pp. 3 f.

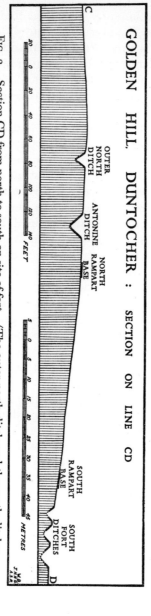

GOLDEN HILL, DUNTOCHER : SECTION ON LINE CD

FIG. 3. Section CD from north to south on site of fort. (The outer north ditch and the south ditches of the fort are put in from trenches cut west of line CD)

The true explanation presented itself in the autumn of 1949, when the " military enclosure " was proved to have been originally a tiny fortlet, less than 60 feet square internally, defended not only by its turf rampart set on a stone base, but also by a steep-sided ditch. This fortlet was the first structure of its kind to be discovered on the line of the Antonine Wall.

To the fortlet, on its east side, had later been added the fort in such a way that the east rampart of the fortlet now served as the west rampart of the fort between the north-west corner of the fort and its west gate. The fortlet ditch was filled in, and the fortlet was retained in use as a small military enclosure outside the west gate of the fort (Fig. 4).

In 1949 evidence was also obtained that at the time when the fort was added to the fortlet the Antonine Wall had still not been completed on the east side of the fort. When the Antonine Wall was at last brought up to the east rampart of the fort it made junction with that rampart at a point about 10 feet south of the north-east corner—farther south, obviously, than the fort-builders anticipated—with the result that the Antonine Wall scraped so closely past the innermost east ditch of the fort that a massive stone buttress had to be built into the ditch-end to prevent the Antonine Wall from subsiding into it.

In its final form, as revealed in the spring of 1951, the fort had had a civil settlement or annexe on its west side, in addition to the military enclosure. The annexe had an internal area almost twice that of the fort itself, and, like the fort, was enclosed by a rampart. The three south ditches of the fort continued along the south side of the annexe, but were reduced to one at the south-west corner of the annexe to leave one ditch only to run along its west side.

The entire north fronts of fort, military enclosure and annexe were covered by the outer north ditch, as well as by the Antonine Ditch. The former ran parallel to the Antonine Ditch for about 420 feet, and then swung southwards at each end to join it.

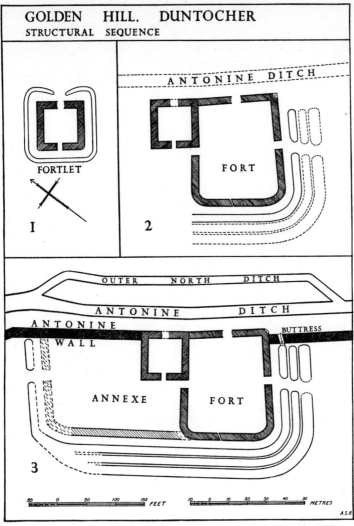

GOLDEN HILL, DUNTOCHER
STRUCTURAL SEQUENCE

ANTONINE DITCH

FORTLET

FORT

1

2

OUTER NORTH DITCH

ANTONINE DITCH

ANTONINE

WALL

BUTTRESS

ANNEXE

FORT

3

50   0   50   100   150 FEET   10   0   10   20   30   40   50 METRES

A.S.R.

Fig. 4. Structural sequence of Antonine works on Golden Hill

A more detailed description of these structural remains now follows, arranged as far as possible in their chronological sequence, and not in the order in which, with difficulty and some incredulity, they were identified.[1] All the pottery found in the excavations could be assigned to the Antonine period.

THE FORTLET

The earliest Antonine structure identified on Golden Hill was a fortlet, lying on the level ground on top of the hill, and overlooking the sweeping southern slope. It occupied indeed the most commanding position on the hill. The fact that it was for a fortlet and not a fort that a site was first chosen probably explains the unusual and awkward position of the fort, which was only later added to the fortlet.

The fortlet measured internally 59 feet from east to west, and 57 feet from north to south. It was defended by a turf rampart set on a stone foundation 12 feet wide, and by a steep-sided V-shaped ditch, 6-7 feet wide and $4\frac{1}{2}$-5 feet deep (Fig. 5). Little of the turf superstructure of the rampart remained in position, but long stretches of the stone foundation survived in an excellent state of preservation. It had two rows of massive squared kerb-stones, with smaller jagged stones packed in between them. Particularly impressive were the remains of the stone base at the northeast corner of the fortlet (Plates 2 and 3). It was in fact the discovery of the neatly finished, outer (east) kerb of the foundation at this corner which first gave rise to the impression that this had once been the outside edge of some structure which had first stood alone and had later had the fort built up against it.

---

[1] It will appear in the detailed plan showing the remains actually uncovered by trenching and found still surviving (Fig. 23) that some of the trenches were not cut at right angles to the defences. This is of course either because the position of the defences was entirely unknown at the time when the trenches were cut or because obstacles in the park at times dictated the direction of the trenches.

The fortlet appeared to have had, from the outset, its two northern corners squared both internally and externally. The stone base at the north-east corner was preserved right up to its north-easterly tip, and the outer east kerb was found to have run straight to the tip. There was no hint that the corner had first been rounded and had then been squared off when the fort rampart was built on to it from the east. The substitution of a right angle for a curve at the inside of the corner would, of course, have had the effect of destroying the inner curve, but at the outside of the corner would have preserved an original curve within the framework of the new right angle. The whole foundation at the outer corner was, however, of uniform build.

The north-west corner was not as well preserved as the north-east corner, but in its latest form had certainly been squared. Here, too, proof was lacking that alterations had ever been made in the foundations at the corner.

The two southern corners did not survive in as good preservation as did the northern corners. Only the inner kerbs were still in position, the outer kerbs having been torn up. The inner corners, in their final form at least, were right-angled, and not rounded. So too must have been the outer corners in their final phase, after the fort was added. For the south-east corner of the fortlet became the north side of the west gateway of the fort, and had to be squared to match the south side of the gateway. Whether, however, the south corners were at first rounded externally and were later squared is now impossible to determine with certainty owing to the poor preservation of the stone base at these corners. Had proof been obtained that the two north corners of the fortlet, in its original form, had been squared externally and the two south corners rounded, that might reasonably have been taken as evidence that, although the fortlet had at first stood alone on the hill, the builders of it had expected that a rampart of some kind would be joined on to its north corners shortly, and so had given these corners a square or straight finish to receive it.

B

Such proof and such evidence were unfortunately not forthcoming.

In spite of this, however, it may be thought likely on general grounds that the fortlet originally had its two southern corners rounded externally. For a turf-walled fortlet of second-century date with all its outer corners squared would be unusual, if not unique, in Roman Britain. Free-standing fortlets or signal-stations of this date elsewhere in Britain, for example at Bowes Moor and Roper Castle in the Stainmore Pass,[1] at Cardurnock (Periods 1 and 2),[2] at Brownhart Law,[3] and Barburgh Mill,[4] at Milton [5] and Durisdeer,[6] appear to have had all their outer corners rounded even although, as for example at Cardurnock, the internal corners may have been squared to accommodate square or rectangular buildings inside.

It may be concluded then that when the fortlet stood alone on the hill, it almost certainly had all its corners squared internally, and had its two north corners also squared externally, but probably, although not certainly, had its two south corners rounded externally—unless, of course, its builders had not only anticipated the addition of a rampart to the two north corners, but had also expected the south-east corner of the fortlet to form part of the west gateway of the later fort and so had squared the south corners externally too. This, however, does not seem very likely.

Even although the addition of other works to the fortlet may have been anticipated from the first, there is no doubt that it had been at first an isolated structure. The fortlet ditch ran round all its four sides.

The ditch was discovered when, in the belief that the

---

[1] Professor I. A. Richmond, in *Aspects of Archæology* (1951), pp. 293 ff.

[2] *Trans. Cumb. and West. A.S.*, n.s. XLVII (1947), pp. 85 ff.

[3] *P.S.A.S.* LXXXIII (1949), pp. 170 ff.

[4] *Trans. Dumfriesshire and Galloway Nat. Hist. and Ant. Soc.*, XXIV (1947), pp. 156 ff.

[5] *The Roman Occupation of South-Western Scotland* (1952), pp. 104 ff.

[6] *Ibidem*, pp. 124 ff.

fortlet was simply a military enclosure attached to the fort, a trench was cut westwards from the east rampart base in an attempt to discover the western limit of the enclosure. The trench disclosed the west rampart base and, about 15 feet outside it, a ditch 7 feet wide and 5 feet deep (Fig. 5). The course of the ditch was followed. It was soon found to have at one time encircled the enclosure, thus proving it to have been originally an independent structure.

In all, over twenty cuttings were made on the line of the fortlet ditch, in order to determine beyond doubt its purpose and direction, and to discover any interruptions in it. The only gap in the ditch was in the north side. It was 20 feet wide. On the other three sides of the fortlet the ditch ran parallel to the rampart and at a distance of 14-15 feet from it, but on the north side the ditch swung in towards the entrance so that although the distance between the ditch and the north corners of the fortlet was 14-15 feet, the distance between ditch and rampart near the north entrance was only 10-11 feet.

The gap in the north ditch of the fortlet was not exactly in the middle of the north side, but very slightly to west of it. A search was made opposite the gap in the ditch for a break in the north rampart and for gate post-holes, but was defeated by the disturbed nature of the remains at this point, and by the restrictions placed on digging through the proximity of a football pitch. Only one small hole, not more than 1 foot in diameter, and less than 1 foot deep, with some scraps of charred wood in it, was located on the line of the north rampart base opposite the gap in the ditch. It might possibly have belonged to the north gate, but it was of a very insignificant nature to have played such a part.[1]

In the south rampart base of the fortlet, on the other hand, there was a clearly defined break, 9 feet wide. Most of the kerb-stones along each side of it were still in position. This

---

[1] See below, p. 23.

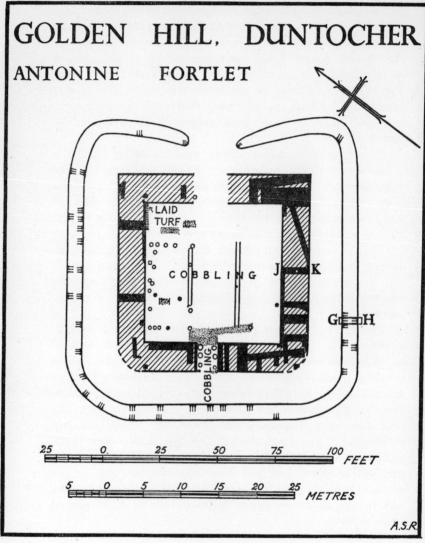

Fig. 5. Plan of fortlet (showing remains actually uncovered)

entrance gap had, along each side of it, three large post-holes. The two most southerly were each 1¼ feet in diameter, and the other four about 2 feet in diameter, so that the actual passage was reduced in width to about 6 feet (Fig. 6). The six post-holes were only roughly circular, with rather ragged edges which hinted at careless digging in Roman times, either when the holes were first dug or possibly when timbers were removed from them. The holes were 1½-2 feet deep, and each had stones in the bottom, but none round about them.

To the south of the easterly row of three post-holes there was a smaller post-hole about 1 foot in diameter and 1 foot deep. To the south of the westerly row of post-holes there were two large stones projecting into the entrance passage as if to form a door stop.

Like the gap in the north ditch, the passage through the south rampart was asymmetrically placed very slightly to the west of the centre of its side of the fortlet. In fact, a line drawn from the mid point of the south entrance parallel to the east and west sides of the fortlet would pass through a point midway between the ends of the north ditch.

This, of itself, suggests that the south gate had been a gate of the fortlet while it stood alone, and had not been made during the period after the fort was built and the fortlet had become simply an adjunct to it. Indeed, had a new gate been made after the fort was in use, it would surely have been placed much nearer to the west gate of the fort, for convenience, rather than more than halfway along the south wall of the military enclosure. Moreover, the posts which had stood in the post-holes must have been massive, flanking a gateway of some strength, and doubtless supporting a superstructure of some kind. They were more suitable, in fact, for the entrance to an isolated fortlet than for the doorway to an enclosure under the protection of a fort. To such a doorway may rather have belonged the small post-hole, and the stones apparently forming a door

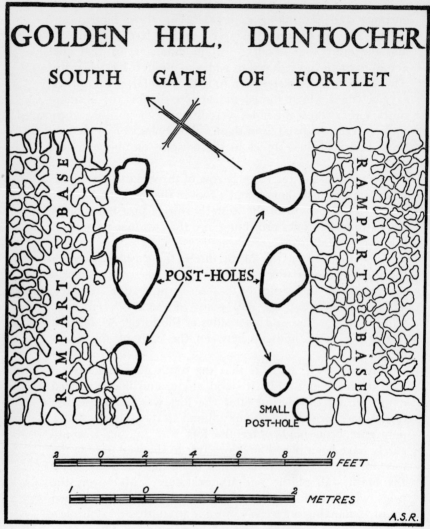

Fig. 6.   Plan of south gate of fortlet

stop, to the south of the large post-holes.[1] That the large post-holes were actually dug at an early stage in the Antonine occupation and were disused later is proved by the fact that they were covered with turf, over which lay a gravelled or cobbled surface, about 1 foot 6 inches thick. From loose soil above the cobbling came a bowl rim,[2] and from below the cobbling came a fragment of olla base,[3] both of Antonine date.

Trenching showed that there was no gap in the ditch opposite the south gate of the fortlet. It was narrow enough of course to have been crossed by a plank bridge. The gap in the north ditch suggests that the main entrance to the fortlet was in the north side. In that case, the north gate should have been of at least as massive a character as the south gate. The single small hole identified near the middle of the north rampart may not have been one of the main post-holes of the north gate, or may possibly have belonged to a smaller gate, in use after the fortlet became an adjunct to the fort. The ground here was so disturbed and digging so restricted that a failure to find large gate post-holes cannot be taken as evidence that there were none there.

There was no gap in the Antonine Ditch opposite the fortlet. If the north gate of the fortlet had remained open and in use after the fort was built and the fortlet became a military enclosure attached to it, any traffic from the enclosure must have been carried across the Antonine Ditch by a bridge, as seems to have happened at the north gate of the fort itself,[4] or else have turned east to cross the Antonine Ditch opposite the north gate of the fort. It is possible, of course, that the north gate of the fortlet was blocked up after the fort was added. No evidence could be obtained for or against this.

Trenching within the fortlet revealed gravelled or

---

[1] There may also have been a direct entry from the fort to the enclosure. See below, p. 33.

[2] See below, p. 85, No. 27.

[3] See below, p. 82 .No. 20h.

[4] See below, p. 47.

cobbled surfaces at many points. Indeed, the whole or most of the internal area appears to have been gravelled or cobbled over at some time during the occupation of the site, but not in its earliest stage, for the cobbled surface within the fortlet was continuous with cobbling which ran through the south entrance and covered the large post-holes there.

Several post-holes were also found within the fortlet, and two long narrow trenches running north and south (Fig. 7). Each trench lay parallel to one of the side walls of the fortlet and exactly 18 feet from it. Both trenches were 1 foot 6 inches to 1 foot 9 inches wide and 6 to 9 inches deep, but the easterly trench was much longer than the westerly trench. Both ends of the latter were located with certainty. It was 24 feet long, and its north end was 18 feet from the north rampart while its south end was 15 feet from the south rampart. Just south of the south end of the trench there was a tiny hole about 4 inches in diameter and 1 foot deep. Into this trench, about 6 feet from its north end, a post-hole had later been inserted.[1]

The easterly trench was traced for at least 36 feet, and may have been longer. Its south end was destroyed by some modern disturbance and its north end lay out of bounds over the edge of a football pitch. At one point in the trench, close to its west edge, and about 22 feet north of the south rampart base, there was a small hole 4 inches in diameter and about 9 inches deep, outlined sharply in the clay subsoil. The edges of both trenches were also sharply and clearly defined, as if something, probably wood, had fitted into them (Fig. 8). If so, perhaps a wooden peg, or tenon, projecting from the underside of a timber or sleeper had produced the small hole in the easterly trench at least.[2] Alternatively, this hole and the other tiny hole south of the westerly trench may have held wooden pegs used in the setting out or in the construction

[1] See below, p. 27.

[2] In this connection it may be noted that the bed plates for the walls of the hut used to shelter the members of the excavating party were bolted into the ground.

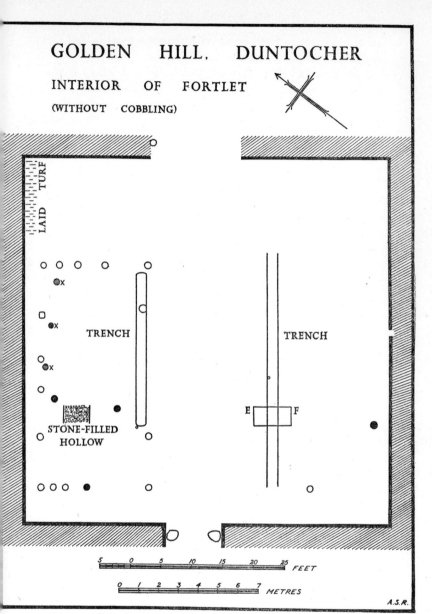

FIG. 7. Plan of remains in interior of fortlet (without cobbling)

of the fortlet. They were contemporary with, or earlier than the trenches, but not later than the trenches.

Both trenches contained much burned clay, flecks of charred wood and ash. From the top of the easterly trench at one point came a fragment of one olla and the base of another.[1] Both trenches were covered by the cobbling which occurred over most of the interior of the fortlet (Figs. 5, 8). They therefore belonged to an early phase of its occupation. From the eastern part of the cobbling, and from loose soil above it, came several amphora fragments, a piece of an urn (?), fragments of ollæ, and of a beaker.[2]

Also belonging to an early phase in the occupation of the fortlet were four post-holes, dug into the clay subsoil. They were each about 1 foot in diameter and 1 foot deep, and were filled with black earth when found. They had lost their packing stones and were wholly or partly covered by gravel or cobbling. One of them, in the south-west corner of the fortlet, had small stones in the bottom. It was not practicable to search the whole internal area of the fortlet for more post-holes corresponding to these four, but their wide distribution over the interior suggests that such post-holes belonged to buildings which occupied a large area of the fortlet.

To a later period must belong the remaining post-holes which had all been dug through made-up soil into the subsoil, had not been covered by cobbling, and which all had packing stones still in or around them. It was only in the western half of the fortlet that it was possible to carry out a systematic search for such post-holes. The eastern half was not fully accessible for excavation.

In the western half of the fortlet, the stone-packed post-holes appeared to outline an area 36 feet long and about 18 feet broad, and had, doubtless, held the upright posts of a wooden building with approximately these dimensions. The north row of post-holes was 16 feet from the north rampart, the south row 5 feet from the south rampart, and the

---

[1] See below, p. 82, Nos. 20a, 20e.

[2] See below, p. 81, Nos. 15c, 18 ; p. 82, Nos. 20b, 20d ; p. 83, Nos. 20k, 20l, 23.

west row 2 feet from the west rampart. The lane between building and rampart was therefore extraordinarily narrow. The west row included six post-holes so placed that the three to the north covered two spans of 8 feet each, and the

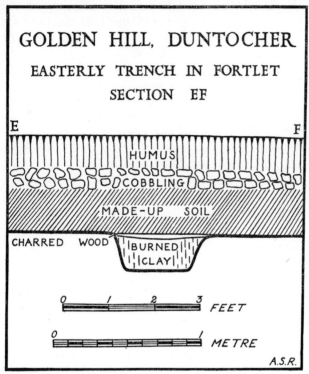

FIG. 8. Section EF across easterly trench in fortlet

three to the south did likewise, leaving between the two sets of three an interval of only 4 feet. Here probably had been a door giving access to the narrow lane between building and rampart. The post-holes in the east row numbered only four, two at the north end with a span of 8 feet between them, the more southerly of these having been inserted into the earlier narrow trench,[1] and two at the south end

[1] See above, p. 24.

with the same span. A stretch of the narrow trench lay between these two sets of post-holes, although the trench had originally belonged to an earlier structure. It is just possible, perhaps, that part of the trench was re-used at one time along with the easterly row of stone-packed post-holes as a bed plate for a sleeper with uprights morticed into it. Yet the trench was covered with gravel, and was not quite in alignment with the post-holes.

The north and south rows of post-holes were not spaced at such regular intervals as were those in the east and west rows. In fact several of them occurred so close together as to encourage the belief that some of them had been dug at a different time from the rest. To a different period from the west row of post-holes too should probably be assigned three odd post-holes lying in a line to the east of the three more northerly post-holes in the west row (Fig. 7, post-holes marked X). The stone packing in the three odd post-holes had collapsed into the holes as if the posts had been withdrawn. In any case, it hardly seemed likely that they had been in use at the same time as the other post-holes in the westerly row.

The post-holes were not all of the same dimensions either. Most of them were 1 foot in diameter and 1-1½ feet deep. The second most northerly post-hole in the west row, however, was 2 feet deep and appeared to have been square in section and lined with stones. The post-holes in the north row were close on 2 feet deep, except for the most easterly post-hole which was 3 feet deep. In loose soil above the north row of post-holes a fragment of Samian (form 18/31 or 31) was found, and from loose soil near the second most southerly post-hole in the west row came an olla fragment.[1]

The wooden building to which the four rows of post-holes belonged had no doubt been subdivided by internal partitions, but no post-holes which might have been associated with such partitions were recovered. The only other feature noted within the area defined by the post-holes was a hollow

---

[1] See below, p. 76, No. 5 ; p. 82, No. 20.

about $4\frac{1}{2}$ feet wide and 1 foot 9 inches deep, filled with stones. The wooden building must, however, have resembled, in dimensions and plan, a wooden barrack building in a Turf Wall milecastle on Hadrian's Wall.[1]

In the east half of the fortlet only one stone-packed post-hole could be identified. It was at the same distance from the south rampart—5 feet—as was the south row of post-holes in the west half of the fortlet, and was the only evidence recoverable which might suggest that a similar wooden building had stood in the east half of the fortlet during at least one period of its occupation.

The only other structural feature noted within the fortlet was a layer of turves just within the north-west corner. Their extent could not be determined but it is possible that they formed part of a corner structure of some kind, like the laid turf inside the north-east corner of the fort.[2]

The structural remains from the interior of the fortlet, so far as they can at present be interpreted, appear then to belong certainly to two, perhaps to more than two, different periods of occupation. To an early period may be assigned the two narrow trenches, and the four post-holes which were filled with heavy black soil and covered with cobbling. Trenches and black-filled post-holes may not of course have been contemporary, but both were certainly of an earlier date than the post-holes which were dug down through made-up soil, were not covered over with cobbling and still had their packing-stones in position. These latter post-holes themselves seem not to be all contemporary with one another, for in several cases pairs of post-holes occurred so close together as to make it seem unlikely that they were in use at the same time. Which of these structural remains belong to the occupation of the fortlet as an isolated post, and which belong to the period after the fort was built will be discussed after the structural remains within the fort have been described.[3]

---

[1] *Trans. Cumb. and West. A.S.*, n.s. xxxv (1935), p. 221.
[2] See below, p. 39.   [3] See below, p. 58.

Meanwhile, it may be said that the fortlet when it stood alone was defended by a turf rampart set on a stone foundation 12 feet wide, and by a steep-sided ditch, 6-7 feet wide, and $4\frac{1}{2}$-5 feet deep, which was interrupted only in the middle of the north side. The north gate must have been the main gate, but there was also an entrance, about 6 feet

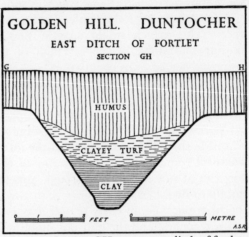

FIG. 9.   Section GH across east ditch of fortlet

wide, in the south side. The south corners were probably rounded externally, but the north corners were squared externally, apparently in the expectation that the fortlet would at some future date be attached to a larger defensive work, either the Antonine Wall or a fort.

Within the fortlet there were probably one or more wooden buildings, set alongside the central road connecting the two gates. To such a wooden building or buildings may have belonged the two narrow trenches, and possibly the black-filled post-holes, later covered with cobbling.[1]

In its dimensions, in the character of its rampart, and perhaps in its internal buildings, the fortlet resembled a milecastle on the Turf Wall sector of Hadrian's Wall. The

[1] But see below, p. 58.

Turf Wall milecastle at High House, for example, measured 66 by 55 feet internally, had a turf rampart, which was, however, 20 feet wide at the base, and squared north corners and rounded south corners. It had two gates, a north gate 12 feet wide and a south gate 10 feet 6 inches wide. Both gates were flanked along each side by posts supporting timber revetments to the rampart ends, and there was a tower over the north gate. There was one barrack block, about 32 feet by 16 feet, on one side of the central roadway.[1]

The time came when the fortlet ceased to stand alone on Golden Hill. Its ditch was filled in. Every section cut across the ditch showed that it had been packed with dark grey clay to a depth of about 2 feet, over which was lighter-coloured clayey turf (Fig. 9). A similar ditch packing was recently noted in the Period I ditch at Cappuck, where Professor Richmond observed that " the whole ditch had been deliberately filled with clay, deposited in recognisable clods or lumps, and sealed over at the top by a harder and cleaner layer." [2] Stretches of the ditch on the west and south sides of the fortlet had stones laid over the clay and clayey turf filling (Fig. 23).

Samples of clay from the Duntocher ditch were submitted to the Royal Botanic Garden, Edinburgh, and were reported by Mr M. Y. Orr to be " clay with quartz containing no recognisable plant remains or charcoal." There had been no growth in the ditch, and little rapid silt in the bottom under the clay packing. This was only to be expected if the ditch had been filled during the continuous occupation of the site and not after a period of abandonment.

Over long stretches of the filled-in fortlet ditch were later laid part of the north rampart base of the fort, part of the west rampart base of the fort immediately south of the west gateway, and buildings of some kind in the north-western sector of the fort.[3] From this area of the fort

[1] *Trans. Cumb. and West A.S.*, n.s. xxxv (1935), pp. 220 ff.
[2] *P.S.A.S.* lxxxv (1951), p. 139.　　　[3] See below, p. 59.

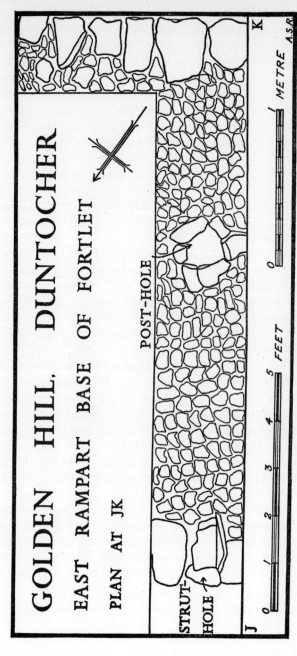

FIG. 10. Plan at JK of east rampart base of fortlet

there may have been a direct entrance into the fortlet. In one section cut across the east rampart base of the fortlet there appeared a post-hole, about 1 foot in diameter and 1 foot deep, at about 4 feet from the east kerb of the base, and a strut-hole inset into the west kerb of the base and slanting up towards the centre of the base (Fig. 10). Clay and burned wood were also present in the loose top soil, along with several small iron nails, a scrap of a semi-cylindrical roofing tile, a fragment of a decorated Samian bowl (form 37) and nine scraps of coarse pottery, six probably from a beaker.[1] Over the base to the north of the post-hole there was a very little turf, and above that was road cobbling. It may be that here the rampart of the fortlet, now a military enclosure attached to the fort, had been breached and a wooden gate-structure inserted in the breach to provide access to the enclosure from the fort. Unfortunately, since this section lay underneath one of the goals of the football pitch, the evidence it yielded could not be fully followed up.

The Fort

The fort was not an exact rectangle (Fig. 23). The northern half of its west side was formed by the east rampart of the fortlet. The southern half of the west side was not in a straight line with the northern half but swung slightly to the west. The north wall of the fort again was not at right angles to the west side but inclined more to the north. The east side of the fort also inclined outwards (to the east) as it ran south, and the south side was not parallel to the north side. The result was that the west side of the fort was slightly shorter than the east side, measuring 156 as against 161 feet internally, and the north side was shorter than the south side, 124 as against 135 feet internally. The fort had an internal area of only about half an acre, and is therefore the smallest known fort on the Antonine Wall.

[1] See below, p. 72, No. 4 ; p. 74, No. 7 ; p. 77, No. 1 ; p. 83, No. 22 ; p. 87, No. 51.

The Rampart. The fort had had a turf rampart set on a stone foundation as did a number of other Antonine Wall forts, for example, at Rough Castle,[1] at Westerwood,[2] at Croy Hill,[3] at Bar Hill,[4] at Cadder,[5] and at Old Kilpatrick.[6] The Antonine fort rampart at Mumrills [7] was of clay, while the forts at Castlecary [8] and Balmuildy [9] were enclosed by stone walls.

At Duntocher, little of the turf superstructure of the rampart survived except at the north-east corner of the fort. Along the north side the rampart was only 12 feet wide at the base, but along the other three sides it was usually over 13 feet wide. Along the north half of the west side of course the east rampart of the former fortlet now served as the rampart of the fort. Here, too, it was only 12 feet wide at the base.

The stone base of the rampart had two outer rows of squared kerb-stones with unshaped stones filling up the whole space between the kerb-stones, and not simply extending inwards from the kerb-stones towards the centre as was the case, for example, at Cadder.[10] The base was best preserved along the east side [11] and in the centre of the south side. Elsewhere, much of it had been destroyed, possibly by the activities of " the same Goth." [12]

Along the southern half of the east side, and on the south side, the sloping ground on which the stone foundation stood had been banked up with turf so that the outer kerbs of the base actually lay over a few courses of turf.

[1] *P.S.A.S.* xxxix (1905), pp. 459 ff. and lxvii (1933), pp. 263 ff.
[2] *P.S.A.S.* lxvii (1933), pp. 280 f.
[3] *P.S.A.S.* lxvi (1932), pp. 247 f.
[4] Macdonald and Park, *The Roman Forts on the Bar Hill* (1906), pp. 20 ff.
[5] John Clarke, *The Roman Fort at Cadder* (1933), pp. 8 f.
[6] S. N. Miller, *The Roman Fort at Old Kilpatrick* (1928), p. 3.
[7] *P.S.A.S.* lxiii (1929), pp. 408 ff.
[8] *P.S.A.S.* xxxvii (1903), pp. 288 ff.
[9] S. N. Miller, *The Roman Fort at Balmuildy* (1923), pp. 7 f.
[10] *Op. cit.*, p. 9.
[11] From loose soil just inside the east rampart-base came a fragment of a Samian platter (form 18/31 or 31). See below, p. 75, No. 4.
[12] See above, p. 4.

A similar levelling of the ground on which a rampart base was to be set was noted at Mumrills,[1] and in the Yorkshire forts of Elslack [2] and Slack.[3] At Mumrills and at Elslack, the levelling material was clay. At Slack it took the form of a layer of sandy soil.

The stone base at the south-east corner of the fort at Duntocher was well enough preserved and was sufficiently examined to determine that this corner had been rounded.[4] At a point west of the corner there were some large squared stones with other squared stones under them, the whole presenting the appearance of having formed one side of a drain (Fig. 23). If there had been a drain here, however, no other remains of it have survived.

No doubt the south-west corner had also been rounded, although the foundation was here too ruinous for this to be established with certainty.[5] At the north-west corner the base had completely disappeared, but it must have made a straight junction with the north-east corner of the fortlet. At the north-east corner the base was not completely preserved to the outermost tip. Its inner corner, however, proved to have been squared. Externally, the corner may at first have been squared too, in anticipation of the junction with it of the Antonine Wall. If so, it was probably rounded off later, when in fact the Antonine Wall made junction with the east rampart of the fort about 10 feet south of the corner, and so left the corner projecting awkwardly to the north (Figs. 21, 23). If the corner was rounded off externally, it would have resembled the north-west corner of the fort at Old Kilpatrick (which was, however, rounded from the first) with the Antonine

[1] *P.S.A.S.* LXIII (1929), p. 409.

[2] Thomas May, *The Roman Forts at Elslack*, in *Yorks. Arch. Journ.* XXI (1911), p. 118.

[3] Dodd and Woodward, *Excavations at Slack*, 1913-15, in *Yorks. Arch. Journ.* XXVI (1922), p. 12.

[4] A bronze pin was found in loose soil over the base at the corner. See below, p. 72, No. 3.

[5] Fragments of a mortarium were found in loose soil over the south-west rampart base just north of the south-west corner. See below, p. 79, No. 4.

Wall running down to it from the north-east.[1] At Duntocher, however, the destruction of the outermost tip of the
north-east corner made it impossible to determine its shape,
either original or ultimate (Plates 4 and 5).[2]

On the south side of the north rampart, and parallel
to it, there lay another stretch of stone foundation, 7 feet
wide, limited on the south by a well-defined kerb. This
stone foundation lay about 7 inches below the level of
the rampart base, and was of an entirely different build
from it. Its kerb included (at a point about 27 feet east
of the north entrance) at least one stone, neatly squared
on all sides, which must previously have been used for
another purpose (Plate 6). Under the 7 feet wide base too
there was made-up soil with small stones in it, and at
two points on either side of the north entrance there
appeared to have been some burned material under it.
Over the base were several courses of laid turf.

There was no doubt that, at some time after the construction of the fort, the north rampart had had built on to
its south side an extension, 7 feet wide at the base, consisting
of a stone foundation with a turf superstructure on top of it.
As only a few courses of turf survived above the stone base
of the extension, it is impossible to say how high it stood.
It may have been added to the north rampart of the fort
on its inner side simply in order to increase its width, like
the 9-10 feet wide extension added to the inside of the fort
rampart on all four sides at Rough Castle.[3] For reasons
given at length in a postscript to his discussion of the
extension at Rough Castle, Sir George Macdonald " set
aside the idea that the extension had been meant to
support a raised walk such as is often found, both at
home and abroad, immediately behind the walls of stone

---

[1] *P.S.A.S.* LXVI (1932), p. 223, Fig. 2.

[2] From loose soil over the stone base at the north-east corner of the fort
came an iron nail, in two pieces, and two pieces of curved tiles, possibly from
semicylindrical roofing tiles. From filling-in in this area came a fragment of
a jug. See below, p. 72, No. 3 ; p. 74, Nos. 8, 9 ; p. 79, No. 11.

[3] *P.S.A.S.* LXVII (1933), pp. 265 ff.

forts erected in the second century or later. The superstructure has, I believe, been of the same height as the
rampart against which it was reared ; it served as a reinforcement pure and simple." [1]   " The intention was to
convert the rampart-top into a more serviceable fighting-
platform by adding to its breadth." [2]

The main reason why Sir George Macdonald discarded
the possibility that the 9-10 feet wide extension to the
rampart at Rough Castle was a " *Wehrgang* " or " sentry-
path " was that " with a rampart that was 20 feet wide at
the base a ' sentry-path ' would have been useless.   To
obtain any view of what lay on the other side, it would be
necessary to clamber on to the rampart itself."   Such an
objection would not, however, operate so strongly at
Duntocher, where the original rampart was only 12 feet
wide at the base, and the extension was only 7 feet wide.

The Duntocher extension may, then, perhaps be
compared with the apparent backing on the inner side
of the stone wall of the fort at Castlecary, which too
was present only on the north side.   The evidence for
the backing at Castlecary took the form of a stone kerb
running parallel to the north fort wall and fully 6 feet
behind it. [3]   Sir George Macdonald was inclined to think
that this kerb marked the edge of a " sentry-path," possibly
of turf, topped by a " duck-board " walk, [4] comparable
to that found at Carnuntum or Lauriacum. [5]   Analogies for
a " sentry-path " or " *Wehrgang* " in combination with a
turf rampart, as distinct from a stone wall, seem, however,
to be lacking, as Mr Clarke has already noted in discussing
the possibility of such a structure at Cadder. [6]   This consideration, and the fact that the stone base of the extension
at Duntocher, although of a different build from the rampart

---

[1] *P.S.A.S.* LXVII (1933), p. 269, and pp. 286 ff.
[2] *R.W.*, p. 223.
[3] *P.S.A.S.* XXXVII (1903), pp. 290 f.
[4] *P.S.A.S.* LXVII (1933), p. 294.
[5] *Der Römische Limes in Oesterreich*, II (1901), pp. 31 f., and XI (1910), p. 5.
[6] John Clarke, *The Roman Fort at Cadder* (1933), p. 14.

base, was yet no less solid, suggest that it was the base of an extension to the rampart intended to increase its width at the top, as at Rough Castle, rather than the base of a " *Wehrgang* " or " sentry-path " some feet lower than the top of the rampart. At Castlecary and at Cadder, the presumed extensions or backings were not laid on a continuous stone base, but if present at all were marked only by a stone kerb or by a raised core of cobbles. At Rough Castle the extension does seem to have been laid on a bottoming which was continuous for long stretches at least.

In any case, whether the extension at Duntocher was a simple thickening of the rampart, or a " sentry-path," it was undoubtedly a secondary addition to the original rampart. Its base lay on made-up soil.

Also, the stone base of the extension was not carried right into the north-east corner of the fort, but stopped 7 feet short of the east rampart (Fig. 23). An area about 7 feet across within the corner was filled with turfwork, at least 2 feet in depth, and laid on natural clay. The turf platform appeared not to be semicircular as would probably have been the case had it been a *ballistarium*, like, for example, the *ballistaria* at Cawthorn [1] and Chew Green.[2] It was apparently square or rectangular and must have been connected with a corner structure of some kind.

A corner tower would, in fact, have been expected here, particularly in view of the expanse of dead ground to the north of the fort. A search for post-holes which might have belonged to such a structure was, however, unrewarding. The only post-hole found was further west, about 5 feet south of the extension. It was about 1 foot in diameter and 1 foot deep, had been neatly packed round with stones and had at least one large stone in it. It was full of soft loose dark soil, in which were found a shapeless piece of rusted iron, a fragment of olla base, and two fragments of a bowl.[3]

---

[1] *Arch. Journ.* LXXXIX (1932), p. 57.   [2] *Arch. Æl.* (4), XIV (1937), p. 139.
[3] See below, p. 73, No. 11 ; p. 82, No. 20g ; p. 85, No. 31.

It is possible that the turfwork was a platform supporting the foot of a staircase to the rampart walk like, for example, the rectangular mass of turf, 8 feet by 6 feet, in the north-east corner of the Turf Wall milecastle at High House,[1] or the turf *ascensus* at Cawthorn.[2] The southern part of the turf platform at Duntocher had streaks of burned clay over it, possibly from a nearby oven,[3] and above that again cobbling. The cobbling was clearly secondary to the turf structure in the corner, but as it did not cover the turfwork completely, but only its southern part, the northern part of the turfwork was probably in use along with the cobbling as well as before it.

Since the turfwork was built in an early period in the occupation of the fort—it was earlier than the cobbling and was moreover laid directly on natural clay—it was almost certainly in existence before the extension to the back of the north rampart, and its presence was doubtless the reason why the extension was not carried right into the north-east corner of the fort.

There was no trace of turfwork surviving within the badly preserved north-west corner of the fort, but it will be remembered that laid turf was present within the north-west corner of the fortlet,[4] later to become a military enclosure attached to the fort. This turfwork may have served the same purpose as the turf platform at the north-east corner of the fort itself.

The Ditches. Careful trenching showed that there had never been any ditches on the west side of the fort, either to the west of the former fortlet (except, of course, the fortlet ditch, now filled in), or outside the southern part of the west rampart. It must have been intended from the first that the ground to the west of the fort should be occupied by an annexe or civil settlement.

Along the north front of the fort ran the Antonine Ditch,

---

[1] *Trans. Cumb. and West. A. S.*, n.s. xxxv (1935), p. 222.
[2] *Arch. Journ.* LXXXIX (1932), p. 31.
[3] See below, p. 61.   [4] See above, p. 29.

20 feet wide. From the north-east corner of the fort [1] to the north-west corner of the fortlet, and for a further 90 feet beyond, the Antonine Ditch was at a constant distance of 20 feet from the north rampart of fort, fortlet or annexe. [2] The north rampart of the fort was not exactly in a straight line with that of the fortlet, and the Antonine Ditch also changed direction slightly at the north-east corner of the fortlet. There is no doubt that the north ramparts of fort and fortlet and the Ditch were intended to run exactly parallel.

The fortlet was of course in existence before the Antonine Ditch. In fact, parts of the north ditch of the fortlet were swallowed up by the digging of the Antonine Ditch. The north rampart of the pre-existing fortlet was therefore there as a guide to the Ditch diggers. Whether the north rampart or rampart base of the fort on the other hand was laid out before the Antonine Ditch was dug is not so certain. The slight change in the direction of the Ditch at the junction of fort and fortlet does not necessarily mean that the fort rampart too was already in existence to dictate the line to be taken by the Ditch. The Ditch may simply have been driven across the hill in the direction of the fortlet and then straightened out to run parallel to its north rampart. [3]

Beyond the Antonine Ditch there was an outer north ditch. The doubling of the Antonine Ditch is a feature not hitherto observed at any other Antonine Wall fort. The addition of two outer ditches to the Antonine Ditch on the west front of the fort at Old Kilpatrick is not exactly analogous, since its position as the terminal fort at the west end of the Wall exposed its west front to attack from the west and no doubt induced the strengthening of its western defences. [4]

The outer north ditch at Duntocher was 14 feet wide

---

[1] From loose soil outside the north-east corner of the fort came a fragment of a mortarium. See below, p. 77, No. 3.

[2] See also below, p. 62.   [3] See below, pp. 47, 100.

[4] *P.S.A.S.* LXVI (1932), pp. 233 ff., and *R.W.*, pp. 334 ff.

and 5-6 feet deep. It was full of natural silt with very dark silt containing rootlets and some scraps of carbonised wood at the bottom (Fig. 11). At some points, its north lip had stones on it, laid in one place over turf.[1] Between the north-east and the north-west corners of the fort it ran exactly parallel to the Antonine Ditch and at a distance of 37 feet from it. Instead of changing direction slightly, however, at the north-east corner of the fortlet, as did the Antonine Ditch, the outer north ditch kept a straighter course, so gradually lessening the distance between itself and that Ditch until at the north-west corner of the fortlet the distance between the two was 36 feet, and 90 feet further west, was 35 feet. Both Antonine Ditch and outer north ditch then inclined slightly northwards.

The total length of the outer north ditch was about 420 feet. It covered the north fronts of fort, fortlet and annexe. Near the north-east corner of the fort, the outer north ditch swung sharply south to join the Antonine Ditch. It did the same at the north-west corner of the annexe.[2] There, the comb between the outer north ditch and the Antonine Ditch had been hardened with clay and small stones.

Along the east and south sides of the fort there ran three ditches. On the east side, the innermost ditch was 14 feet wide and at least 5 feet 3 inches deep. The middle ditch was 13 feet wide and at least 5 feet deep, and the outermost ditch was 20 feet wide and at least 4 feet deep.

The waterlogged nature of the ground made it difficult to obtain good sections of the east ditches, but the evidence recovered indicated that they were steep-sided rather than gently V-shaped. The berm between the east rampart and the innermost east ditch was cobbled or gravelled, at least on the north side of the east gate. The cobbling of a berm has been noted elsewhere, for example at Slack.[3]

---

[1] See below, p. 67.   [2] See below, p. 62.
[3] Dodd and Woodward, *Excavations at Slack*, 1913-15, in *Yorks. Arch. Journ.*, xxvi (1922), p. 17.

The bank between the second and third ditches had also been hardened with large cobbles, and, in one section at least, the bank between first and second ditches.

After rounding the south-east corner, the three ditches assumed slightly different dimensions. The innermost south ditch was 13 feet wide, the middle south ditch was 14 feet wide and the outermost south ditch was 16 feet wide. Here too, owing to the presence of modern drains, good sections were impossible to obtain, but such evidence as was forthcoming suggested that the ditches were of normal V-shaped profile (Fig. 3).

An interesting feature revealed itself in sections cut across the innermost south ditch. The scarp and the ground to north of it had been banked up with turf laid over clay and hardened with large cobbles, in order no doubt to increase the depth of the ditch, and the difficulty of getting out of it, on a steep slope. The rampart base on this slope, it has already been noted, had had its south edge laid on turf.[1] This was continuous with the turf on the scarp of the innermost south ditch.

Along both south and east sides the ditches ran exactly parallel to the rampart. The berm between the rampart base and the innermost ditch was 13½-14 feet wide,[2] and the banks between each pair of ditches had a constant width of 3 feet.

As they approached the north-east corner of the fort, the three east ditches came to rounded ends. The two outermost ditches stopped 30 feet south of the corner, and the innermost ditch about 28 feet south of it. Ample space was thus left for the Antonine Wall to make junction with the east fort rampart at or just south of the corner.

In fact, the Antonine Wall did not do so. For some reason, either in order to maintain a constant interval

---

[1] See above, p. 34.

[2] From loose soil above the south berm came a piece of curved tile, a Samian fragment, the base of a jug (?) and a bowl-rim. See below, p. 74, No. 10 ; p. 76, No. 9 ; p. 80, No. 14 ; p. 85, No. 33.

between the Antonine Wall and Ditch of about 30 feet on the east side of the fort, or for some other reason that cannot now be recovered, the Antonine Wall made junction with the east rampart of the fort about 10 feet south of the north-east corner. In so doing it scraped so closely past the innermost east ditch of the fort that a great stone buttress had to be built into the ditch-end to prevent the Antonine Wall from subsiding into it. The buttress lay partly under the Antonine Wall base, and was constructed of stones at least as massive as those of the Wall base. The buttress projected over 2 feet to the south of the Wall base and measured 7 feet 7 inches from east to west, and went down at least 6 feet into the ditch-end (Plate 7).

The other two east ditches were not so closely skirted by the Antonine Wall, and were not provided with buttresses. It was noted, however, that stone packing had been rammed in between the Antonine Wall and the middle east ditch.

The Entrances. The north side of the west entrance of the fort was formed by the south-east corner of the fortlet. Between this corner and the sector of the fort rampart which ran along the south half of the west front of the fort there was a space of 13 feet. This was the site of the west gateway. It was very slightly to the north of the middle of the west side of the fort.

As has been said, the rampart base at the south-east corner of the fortlet, that is on the north side of the west gateway, was in poor preservation.[1] No trace survived of kerbs defining the edge of the rampart at this point. On the south side of the gateway, however, kerb-stones and parts of the stone base of the rampart were found *in situ*, in a position which indicated that the rampart had ended with a straight edge on this side of the entrance passage. There had not been a recess at the inner end of the entrance passage. The north side of the passage almost certainly must have had a straight edge too.

A search was made for post-holes along the sides of the

[1] See above, p. 17.

west gate-passage and within the fort on either side of the gate. No post-holes were found in these positions. There did, however, come to light the remains of a well-built drain running through the entrance passage. It was $1\frac{1}{2}$ feet across internally and 1 foot 3 inches deep, and its sides were formed of stones carefully set one on top of the other (Fig. 23). No doubt it had been covered by flagstones but none of these survived. The drain ran parallel to the north side of the gate-passage and at a distance of 2 feet from it. A box-culvert of almost exactly the same dimensions as this drain, but with its cover slabs intact, and in a similar position, has recently been found at the south-east gateway of the fort at Neath, Glamorganshire.[1]

The Duntocher drain or culvert was traced for 14 feet right through the passage from the inner to the outer edge. At the outer edge of the passage, the drain made a right-angled turn south. A stretch of only 5 feet of the southward branch of the drain survived, but it was recognised that its continuation southwards in a straight line would carry it alongside the outer kerb of the west rampart of the fort on the south side of the west gateway. A trench cut just over 20 feet south of the gateway across the outer kerb of the stone base of the rampart did in fact reveal a further length of drain. Its east edge was formed by the outer kerb of the base and its west edge was formed of laid stones. It exactly resembled the drain in the gate passage and was no doubt connected with its southward branch. It probably had an outlet into the innermost south ditch outside the west rampart of the fort.

In the west gate-passage too there were many patches of cobbling—all that survived of a road through the gateway. There appeared in fact to be more than one level of cobbling, as if the road had been relaid or repaired or resurfaced.

In its course westwards the road must have sent off a branch into the military enclosure by way of its south gate. Cobbling was in fact present in the entrance to the

[1] *Bulletin of Board of Celtic Studies*, XIV (1953), p. 78.

enclosure, and also over the filled-in south ditch of the fortlet.

The stone base of the north fort rampart was so badly preserved that it was difficult to determine where exactly it had been interrupted by a gate-passage. Persistent trenching, however, finally revealed the fact that, near the middle of the north side of the fort, there was a cobbled gap, 14 feet wide, with some large laid stones on either side of it. The cobbling must represent the remains of a road through the north gateway, although not of the first such road, for the cobbling lay over ash and some other unidentified, burned material, with which were a fragment of a mortarium, and another of a bowl rim.[1] The road through the north gate had been wholly or partly relaid over occupation debris.

The large laid stones on either side of the road cobbling were all that survived of the stone base under the rampart ends flanking the gate passage, and of the stone base of the southward extension to the rampart. Fortunately these laid stones, which included a few kerb-stones, were so located as to indicate that the north gate-passage had been straight-sided without any recesses. The passage lay a little to the east of the centre of the north side of the fort.

No post-holes were identified in the actual gate-passage, but there was one, about 1 foot in diameter and 1 foot deep, behind the rampart base just to the west of the passage, and there was another, of the same dimensions, to the east of the gate passage and about 7 feet south of the north rampart base, that is immediately south of the extension to the north rampart. It is possible that these post-holes held posts which helped to support stairs to the rampart top on either side of the gateway, or that on the other hand they were connected with small guard-chambers attached to the south side of the rampart ends on either side of the gateway. Guard-chambers in such a position behind a turf rampart

[1] See below, p. 77, No. 3a ; p. 85, No. 36.

were present, for example, at Old Kilpatrick,[1] and at the east and south gates of the fort at Cadder.[2]

At Duntocher, unfortunately, it remains uncertain whether the two identifiable post-holes, one on either side of the north entrance, were connected either with stairs to the rampart walk or with guard-chambers. It is not even certain that the post-holes were contemporary. The post-hole west of the entrance lay south of the rampart base, but within the extension, although admittedly not covered by the base of the extension, while the post-hole east of the entrance lay south of the extension. What does, however, seem reasonable or likely is that at the north gate there must have been, if not a gate-tower, at least one guard-house with an upper storey giving a view over the level ground to the north, and some means of reaching the level of the rampart walk either from the upper storey of a guard-house or by a separate staircase.

The failure to identify gate post-holes at this or indeed at any of the three fort gateways is most strange in view of the fact that post-holes were found, for example, at the south gate of the fortlet, as well as at various points within the fort and fortlet. It may possibly be due to the particularly disturbed nature of the ground round about the fort gateways, and to limitations set on digging. Gateways without deep-set gateposts would be hard to envisage.

The Antonine Ditch was not interrupted opposite the fort. This was established with certainty by the digging of sections across it at frequent intervals along the whole north front (Fig. 23). The only other Antonine Wall forts (so far as is known) opposite which there were no breaks in the Antonine Ditch were at Croy Hill and Westerwood. At Croy Hill, it is true, a gap had been left in the Ditch to the east of the fort, although there was none opposite the north gateway.[3] At Westerwood, however, the Ditch

[1] S. N. Miller, *The Roman Fort at Old Kilpatrick* (1928), p. 15.
[2] John Clarke, *The Roman Fort at Cadder* (1933), pp. 18 ff.
[3] *P.S.A.S.* LXVI (1932), p. 247.

ran straight past the fort. This, Sir George Macdonald believed, indicated that the Antonine Ditch had been dug before the fort was built.[1]

At Duntocher too, it may be that although the Antonine Wall certainly did not arrive until after the fort was built, yet the Antonine Ditch came earlier than the fort and so ran across the hill without a break. So little is known of the working arrangements of the legionary squads on the Antonine Wall that there is no sure ground for assuming that a squad which built a certain stretch of the Wall was responsible also for digging the same stretch of the Ditch. Nor yet, moreover, can it be assumed that Wall builders and Ditch diggers always worked exactly neck and neck, whether they came from the same squad or not.

If at Duntocher the Antonine Ditch came earlier than the fort, then the fact that the Ditch and the north rampart of the fort were exactly parallel would have to be explained on the assumption that the rampart was laid down parallel to a pre-existing Ditch and not *vice versa*. The slight change in the direction of the Antonine Ditch at the north-east corner of the fortlet would then have dictated a slight change in the direction of the north fort rampart and so have caused it to diverge slightly from the line of the north rampart of the earlier fortlet.[2]

Since there was no interruption in the Antonine Ditch, the road from the north gateway must have been carried across it by a timber bridge, although no trace of such a bridge was found. Bridges over ditches which were at least as wide as this stretch of the Antonine Ditch—20 feet— were, however, required on other sites (besides Westerwood),[1] for example at the west gate of the fort at Cadder, at least until part of the ditch was filled in,[3] and at the north gate of the fort at Slack,[4] where there was a double ditch over 20 feet

---

[1] *P.S.A.S.* LXVII (1933), p. 280.

[2] See above, p. 40, and below, p. 100.

[3] John Clarke, *The Roman Fort at Cadder* (1933), pp. 22 ff.

[4] Dodd and Woodward, *Excavations at Slack*, 1913-15, in *Yorks. Arch. Journ.*, XXVI (1922), p. 15.

wide, the inner part of which had a level step which may have helped to support a bridge.

The presence of a football pitch made it impossible to cut trenches across the line of the outer north ditch opposite the north gateway of the fort, or indeed to cut trenches frequently enough along its line anywhere, to determine whether or not there had been any gaps in that ditch, to allow a road or roads to pass through. Since, however, the Antonine Ditch was not interrupted anywhere along the north front of either fort, fortlet or, apparently, annexe, it does not seem likely that the outer north ditch was interrupted either.

There was a gap of $13\frac{1}{2}$ feet in the east rampart base, a little to the north of the middle of the east side. The kerb along the edge of the rampart on the south side of this entrance passage was preserved for its whole length, $13\frac{1}{2}$ feet, and that on the north side partly so. They showed that the east rampart had ended with a straight edge on either side of the passage, without any recesses.

No post-holes could be identified along the rampart ends on either side of the gate-passage, or on the inner side of it, possibly because of the disturbed and waterlogged nature of the ground. Much road cobbling, however, was noted in the passage, and to the east of it. Rather smaller cobbling was also found in every trench cut across the berm between the east rampart and the inner east ditch, from the east gateway northwards in the direction of the north-east corner of the fort. It appeared that the whole space between rampart and ditch from the east gateway northwards had been cobbled for some purpose. No cobbling was noted in the corresponding space to the south of the east gateway.

All three east ditches were interrupted at the east entrance. The gap in the innermost ditch was 17 feet wide, as was also that in the middle ditch. Both these ditches had rounded ends but the ends on the south side of the entrance were much blunter than those on the north. The gap in the innermost ditch was not exactly opposite the gateway through the rampart, but lay more than 5 feet to the south of it. The gap in the middle ditch lay 4 feet south again from that in the innermost ditch.

The exact position of the gap in the outermost ditch could not be ascertained exactly as the ground here was scarred and criss-crossed by modern field drains. Two points near the end of the ditch on the south side of the entrance, and another near its end on the north side of the entrance were, however, established. A trench cut midway between ran across undisturbed ground, thus proving that the ditch had been interrupted. The conjectural endings given to the outermost ditch on the plan are based on the assumption that the entrance gap in it measured 17 feet as did that in the other two east ditches, and on the supposition that the gap in the outermost ditch lay as far to the south of that in the middle ditch (that is, 4 feet) as the gap in the middle ditch lay to the south of that in the innermost ditch.

However that may be, the position of the gateway through the rampart, and of the gaps in the innermost and middle ditches, suffice to indicate that a road had not run straight in through the east ditches and gate, but had approached obliquely from the south-east. Similar oblique approaches were indicated by the gateways and ditch-ends at certain other Antonine Wall forts too, for example, at the west gate at Mumrills,[1] at the west gate at Croy Hill,[2] at the west gate at Balmuildy [3] and apparently at the east gate at Old Kilpatrick.[4]

Road cobbling was still present in the gap between the ends of the innermost east ditch. It extended over the whole width of the gap, 17 feet, and no definite edges or kerbs to it could be identified. There was, however, discovered a stretch of cobbling extending northwards over part of the end of the innermost ditch on the north side

[1] *P.S.A.S.* LXIII (1929), pp. 415 ff.
[2] *P.S.A.S.* LXVI (1932), p. 249 and Pl. x.
[3] S. N. Miller, *The Roman Fort at Balmuildy* (1922), p. 21 and Pl. LVIII.
[4] *P.S.A.S.* LXVI (1932), pp. 235 f. and Fig. 5.

D

of the entrance. There did appear to be a north edge to the cobbling, like the edge of a road, which from its direction looked as if it was coming in from the north-east, and in so doing running across all three east ditches. A south edge to the cobbling could not be found, however— it simply tailed off—and the sodden nature of the ground prevented any attempt to discover whether there was any filling in the ditch-end under the cobbling. Two amphora fragments, however, were found just under the cobbling.

Apart from this short stretch of cobbling across the end of the innermost ditch on the north side of the entrance gap, no other evidence for a road from the north-east was found. The cobbling over the ditch-end may perhaps have served some other purpose not now obvious.

There was no gate in the south side of the fort. When that was first suspected, as a result of trenches cut across the rampart base near the middle of the south side, a continuous stretch of the stone base, 50 feet long, was uncovered in this area in order to determine beyond doubt whether it had ever been interrupted. There was no evidence that there had been a break in the middle of the south rampart at any time. The stones of which the base was composed were all of the same massive character. Trenches were also cut across the base on either side of the 50 feet stretch, but without discovering any interruption in it.

On the other hand, the rampart base in the middle of the south side had had incorporated in it a drain or gutter running across the base from north to south (Fig. 23). It was over 1 foot in width, and almost 1 foot deep, and its sides were formed of very large squared stones, almost as massive as those of the base itself. There were no cover slabs surviving. Close to the gutter, and just inside the rampart base, in top soil, there were found a piece of modern piping [1] and a piece of a mortarium.[2]

Further, almost exactly at the mid point of the south side of the fort, about 6 feet west of the gutter, there pro-

---

[1] See below, p. 73, No. 12 ; pp. 123 ff.   [2] See below, p. 79, No. 9.

jected into the fort from the inner kerb of the stone base a stone-built platform 6 feet long and 5 feet wide. It was edged on north and south sides by very massive stones (Fig. 22 and Plate 8) and seemed to overlap the rampart base very slightly. It may not, however, be later than the base, as it stood on natural clay.

The presence of the stone platform at that point showed clearly enough that there was no entrance there, but its purpose was not so clear. It was somewhat similar to stone flagging, 12 feet long by 10 feet 6 inches wide, found inside the north-east gate of the fort at Haltwhistle,[1] but was of course much smaller in extent. It was too small, in fact, to have been the floor of a tower.

It did not present the features of a *ballistarium* either. *Ballistaria* seem to have been usually semicircular mounds of turf, as at Cawthorn, where they were 8 feet in diameter,[2] and at Chew Green.[3] There was no trace of turfwork on top of the stone platform at Duntocher. It may rather have been the base of an *ascensus* of some kind, perhaps a flight of wooden steps leading to the rampart walk. At Cawthorn, an *ascensus* on the east side of the south gate took the form of " a rectangular extension of the back of the rampart, six feet square." [4] This was similar in size to the stone platform at Duntocher.

To the north of the stone platform, there was much evidence of burning. Abundant ash, charcoal, burned clay, and some small calcined stones were present. Among the stones were two fragments of a mortarium and part of an olla base.[5] There was no shape to the burned clay, but the impression given by the burned remains was that they had come from an oven nearby, or at least from a hearth.

There was no interruption in the three south ditches opposite the middle of the south side of the fort. This

[1] *Arch. Æl.* (3), v (1909), p. 249.
[2] *Arch. Journ.*, LXXXIX (1932), p. 57.
[3] *Arch. Æl.* (4), XIV (1937), p. 139.
[4] *Arch. Journ.*, LXXXIX (1932), p. 31.
[5] See below, p. 79, No. 10a ; p. 82, No. 20c.

was only to be expected in the absence of a south gate. Its absence was probably due to the extreme steepness of the southern slope and to the difficulty there would have been in bringing wheeled traffic up it into the fort. The earlier antiquaries, Gordon, Horsley and Roy,[1] although wrong in placing a gate in the south side of the fort, were no doubt right in making the Military Way skirt the southern defences, although no trace of such a road can now be seen on the ground. Horsley was even correct in making the Military Way send off a branch to enter the east gate of the fort. The ditch-endings at that gate indicate the direction from which such a branch made its approach. They suggest, too, that in all probability the Military Way was already in existence when the fort was built. If not, the diggers of these fort ditches certainly knew or anticipated that the Military Way would skirt the fort. Indeed, they could hardly have expected anything else, since the fort was so small.

Streets inside the fort. Cobbling was found immediately inside the ramparts on all four sides of the fort. This must represent the remains of the *intervallum* street, but at no point, unfortunately, was it possible to discover the exact breadth of the street.

It was, however, remarked that in certain places, at least, notably behind the north rampart, it was possible to distinguish two levels of cobbling. Behind the north rampart, moreover, the uppermost cobbling had on it a piece of brick [2] (which may, however, not be Roman), and lay over burned material, as did the street running through the north gateway.[3] In the north-east corner, too, the high level cobbling lay over the southern end of a platform of laid turf.[4]

The only other street within the fort of which certain traces were found was that between the east and the west gateways. Cobbling of this street was found just inside

---

[1] See above, p. 3.   [2] See below, pp. 73, 127.
[3] See above, p. 45.   [4] See above, p. 39.

these two gateways, and at about the mid point of the fort. At this point, there was a considerable depth of cobbling, about 1 foot in thickness, but it was not possible to distinguish separate layers in it.

Structures inside the fort. Excavation within the fort was extremely restricted and those remains which were discovered proved to have been seriously disturbed, probably by the activities of " the same Goth " [1] and others of like mind. Trenching of a limited area in the centre of the southern half of the fort did, however, disclose stretches of the stone foundations of a long narrow building. The foundations were $2\frac{1}{2}$-3 feet wide, and were bordered by neatly laid stones with straight edges. Between them were smaller stones.

The foundations outlined a building 62 feet long by 22 feet broad externally. It was divided laterally by another foundation which lay about 20 feet south of the north foundation. The building was further divided longitudinally by a central foundation. At least one other fragment of foundation was found about 20 feet north of the south foundation. It ran westwards from the central foundation to the outer west foundation (Fig. 22).

There may have been other internal divisions in the building, but no traces of these survived. There were no remains either of the actual walls of the building, nothing to determine with certainty whether they had been of stone or of wood. In view, however, of the fact that post-holes (of more than one period) were in use immediately to east of the long narrow building, presumably to hold the uprights of wooden buildings,[2] it seems more likely that the stone foundations of the long narrow building had been the foundations of stone walls, rather than the stone sills of wooden walls.

The position of a doorway or doorways in the long building is also uncertain. The poor preservation of the foundations made it impossible to be certain whether

---

[1] See above, p. 4.   [2] See below, p. 57.

D 2

interruptions in them were of ancient or modern origin, and whether they were deliberate or accidental.

Along the north edge of the long narrow building there was a gutter, over 1 foot wide, and apparently in line with the gutter running through the west gate of the fort.[1] North of the gutter was road cobbling.

The long narrow building occupied approximately the position usually reserved, in a fort, for the Headquarters Building, or Principia. Like the rather larger building, 70 feet by 60 feet, found in a somewhat similar position in the rather larger fort at Cappuck, " it turned out, however, to possess features which make it very doubtful whether this name can be applied to it." [2] The Duntocher building in fact resembled, disconcertingly, a barrack block more than a Principia.

A fort as tiny as that at Duntocher could not, of course, have accommodated a Principia of anything like normal size or plan. Headquarters Buildings in Antonine Wall forts ranged in size from that of the first Antonine period at Mumrills, which measured 119 feet by 100 feet (over half the size of the whole fort at Duntocher),[3] to that at Croy Hill, which measured 61 feet by $67\frac{1}{2}$ feet,[4] with a still smaller Headquarters Building at Rough Castle, the second smallest fort on the Antonine Wall (so far as is known).

The Headquarters Building at Rough Castle, described specifically as the Principia on an inscribed tablet found within it, is nearest in dimensions and outline, although not in internal plan, to the long narrow building at Duntocher. It measured 75 feet from north to south by 44 feet from east to west, and appeared to have had three courtyards and a range of three small rooms at the back.[5] It may be that at Duntocher a building of even more unusual plan had to serve as an administrative centre, owing to the cramped conditions within the fort, for there must surely

---

[1] See above, p. 44.
[2] *P.S.A.S.* XLVI (1912), p. 460.
[3] *P.S.A.S.* LXIII (1929), pp. 421 ff.
[4] *P.S.A.S.* LXXI (1937), p. 37.
[5] *P.S.A.S.* XXXIX (1905), pp. 470 ff., *R.W.* pp. 226 ff.

have been an administrative centre or at least a unit office.

The few finds from the area of the long building did not give any clue to its purpose. They comprised twelve fragments of an urn found in burned material beside its west wall, a fragment of an urn found in loose soil just west of the building, and a bowl fragment from loose soil above the north end of the building.[1]

Whatever its purpose, the long building had not been the earliest building to occupy a central position in the fort. The long building lay parallel to the south and west ramparts of the fort, and was certainly flanked by a cobbled or gravelled alley running along its east side, and probably by another on its west side. The gravelled alley to east of the building, on being examined carefully, proved to have been laid over the stone foundations of an earlier building which was smaller than the long building and had a slightly different alignment. Its east foundation lay exactly parallel to the east rampart of the fort. East and west ramparts, it will be remembered, were not parallel to one another.[2]

The east foundation of the small building, part of the south foundation and the north foundation were all preserved (Fig. 22). The north foundation appeared to have been incorporated in the north foundation of the later, superimposed long building. As the two buildings, and consequently the two north foundations, were on a slightly different alignment, the outer (north) kerbs of the two north foundations did not coincide exactly, but diverged slightly from one another.

It was noted that the north foundation of the small building would lie parallel to, and just on the edge of, a road from the east to the west gateways. The north foundation of the long narrow building, on the other hand, was not parallel to such a road but must have interrupted its direct course from one gate to the other.

The foundations of the earlier, small building were

---

[1] See below, p. 81, Nos. 15, 16 ; p. 86, No. 37.   [2] See above, p. 33.

2½-3 feet wide, and from north to south the building measured 28 feet long externally, and from east to west at least 23 feet across externally. Its west foundation was not discovered.

For the reason given above in the discussion of the overlying long building,[1] the foundations of the small building were more likely to have been the foundations of stone walls than the stone sills for timber walls. Its position too, like that of the long building above it, was that usually occupied by a Headquarters Building, but it was of surprisingly small size if it ever served such a purpose. The nearest parallels to the small building seem to be the two stone buildings, 31 feet by 31 feet 6 inches and 28 feet square respectively, on Sites 1 and 111 at Haltwhistle.[2] Nothing, unfortunately, was found inside either of these latter buildings which gave a clue to their use, and neither of them occupied a position in or near the centre of the fort.

Whatever was the purpose of the small squarish building and of the superimposed long narrow building at Duntocher, there is no doubt that they represent two distinct phases of the occupation of the fort, within the Antonine period, as do the north rampart and its extension,[3] and the two layers of cobbling on certain streets and roads.[4] Further evidence for at least two Antonine occupations came from the southern part of the long building. Its foundations here had been laid on a considerable depth of made-up soil, measuring at least 1 foot, sometimes as much as 2 feet, in depth. This made-up soil contained occupation debris— stones, burned clay, charred wood, ash, etc. At one point, below the occupation debris, there was detected a stretch of a trench or hollow, about 2 feet wide and cut into the natural clay (Fig. 22).

It was not, of course, surprising to find that the ground had been made up to provide a more level bed for the stone foundations of the southern part of the long building. The

---

[1] See above, p. 53.   [2] *Arch. Æl.* (3), v (1909), pp. 251 f.
[3] See above, p. 38.   [4] See above, pp. 44 f., 52.

steepness of the slope here dictated that (Fig. 3). But the fact that the made-up soil contained occupation debris covering an earlier trench or hollow showed that there had been an occupation of this part of the site, south of, and no doubt contemporary with, the small squarish building, before the construction of the long narrow building.

Evidence for two periods of occupation presented itself in a different form to the east of the central buildings. Here, exploratory trenches revealed the existence of post-holes belonging to two different periods. To the earlier period belonged three post-holes, each about 1 foot in diameter and about 1 foot deep, and each filled with heavy black ashy soil. They had no packing stones round them, but the most southerly hole had small stones in the bottom. These three post-holes were in line with one another, their line being parallel to that of the small early building, and at a distance of about 3 feet from it (Fig. 22).

To a later period belonged two post-holes, also about 1 foot in diameter and 1 foot deep, which still had their packing stones in position. One of these stone-packed post-holes was so close to one of the black-filled post-holes that they could hardly have been in use together. The structure to which the two stone-packed post-holes belonged appeared to lie parallel to the long narrow building, and at a distance of 12 feet from it (Fig. 22). In loose soil south of these post-holes there were two bowl fragments.[1]

Other three post-holes in the southern half of the fort, to the east of the central buildings, also had their packing stones in position. They were each about 1 foot in diameter, and $1\frac{1}{2}$ feet deep (Fig. 23).

All these stone-packed post-holes were presumably contemporary, having been in use during the latest occupation of the fort. They probably belonged to wooden barrack blocks, but circumstances did not permit of a search for others in the series which would have thrown light on their plan.

It will have been noted that black-filled post-holes and

[1] See below, p. 86, No. 39.

stone-packed post-holes were present in both the fort and the fortlet. If, as seems likely, the black-filled post-holes in both fort and fortlet were contemporary with one another, and the stone-packed post-holes in both fort and fortlet were also contemporary with one another, there then remains nothing so far identified within the fortlet which can be assigned to the period when it stood alone before the fort was built, except the two lengths of narrow trench.[1]

It will be remembered, too, that the stone-packed post-holes within the fortlet appeared to include pairs of post-holes so close together that they could hardly have been in use at the same time, and that certain members of these pairs had their packing stones collapsed into them as if the posts had been withdrawn and had not been left standing (Fig. 7).[2] No such features were noted in connection with the stone-packed post-holes in the fort, but only a few of these, of course, could be identified. It was only in the fortlet that any hint was forthcoming that there might have been three Antonine periods of occupation (in addition to the occupation of the fortlet as an isolated structure), the black-filled post-holes representing the first Antonine period, and the stone-packed post-holes relating certainly to one, and possibly to two, subsequent periods.[3]

Other structural remains found within the area of the fort were slight indeed. Among them were ill-preserved sections of stone foundations to east of the central buildings (Fig. 23). In loose soil just west of these foundations were two mortarium fragments, two fragments of an urn (?), and six pieces of bowls.[4]

To east and south of the central buildings there was some cobbling, and south of them there were several gulleys or hollows containing stones, much soot or charcoal, and at one point some soot-blackened amphora fragments. There was at least one fireplace behind the south rampart. There

---

[1] See above, p. 29, and below, pp. 91 f.   [2] See above, p. 28.
[3] See above, p. 29.
[4] See below, p. 79, No. 10b ; p. 81, No. 15a ; p. 86, Nos. 38, 42.

was much evidence of burning there, and near the stone
platform attached to the south rampart,[1] and also to the
west of the central building (Fig. 22).

From loose top soil in the southern part of the fort came
many potsherds. They comprised amphora fragments,
including the rim and a piece of the body of an amphora
with an incised cross, a piece of a mortarium, fragments of a
mortarium of very slight character, a fragment of an olla,
and pieces of a bowl.[2]

In the north-west sector of the fort, over the filled-in
fortlet ditch, there were found clusters of large stones, one
extending for at least 6 feet and then tailing off, too disturbed to be translated now into the plan of a building.
In and around the stones were found charcoal, burned clay
or daub, two iron nails, two pieces of brick, two tile fragments, and some potsherds—a mortarium rim and fragments,
two pieces of an olla, and two bowl fragments.[3]   Further
east, a small bronze object turned up in loose soil.[4]

In the north-east sector of the fort, just inside the east
rampart, there was an oven, much ruined (Fig. 23).   The
oven had been roughly circular, its internal diameter being
about 7 feet.   It had been enclosed by rough stone walling
of which little still survived, and it had had a flagged
floor.   No trace of either a hob or a flue remained.   In and
around the oven lay much burned clay and charred wood,
showing that the oven had been fuelled with wood and had
had a dome of clay, or of rubble and clay.   One piece of
clay from the oven area may bear the impress of a wooden
post.[5]   The dome had probably been of beehive shape,
with a hole in the top to serve as a chimney.[6]

Also in and around the oven were found a bronze stud
or dress-fastener, iron scraps, a piece of brick (from the

[1] See above, p. 51.

[2] See below, p. 77 ; p. 79, Nos. 8, 10 ; p. 83, No. 20j ; p. 85, No. 35.

[3] See below, p. 72, Nos. 1, 2 ; p. 73 ; p. 74, Nos. 19, 20 ; p. 79, No. 5 ;
p. 82, No. 20f ; p. 85, No. 32 ; p. 86, No. 36a ; pp. 127 f.

[4] See below, p. 71, No. 2.   [5] See below, p. 73.

[6] For a discussion of small Roman ovens see P.S.A.S. LXXVI (1942), pp. 119 ff.

filling-in), four tile fragments, and many potsherds. There were six fragments of a Samian bowl (form 37), an amphora base, the base of a jug (?), a fragment of an urn, fragments of an olla, a piece of a platter, fragments of two bowls, four pieces of a lid, and two fragments of a red pedestal vessel.[1] Finally, upside-down on the flagged floor of the oven, lay the greater part of a Samian platter (form 31 R).[2]

The oven at Duntocher occupied a normal situation for an oven, just behind the fort rampart. In position, in size and in shape and structure, it resembled many other military ovens, for example, the three ovens within the west rampart at Bar Hill,[3] the oven inside the south fort wall at Balmuildy,[4] the four ovens in a row behind the east rampart at Birrens,[5] the oven inside the north-east corner of the small fort at Haltwhistle,[6] and the very well preserved oven inside the east angle of the inner fort at Castleshaw.[7]

The manner in which such ovens were used is clear from their shape and the wood found inside them. " A fire would be kept blazing in the interior, fanned by the prevailing, westerly, wind blowing along the flue, until the oven walls and dome had been heated to the required temperature. The fire would then be allowed to die down and the ashes be raked out by way of the flue, the raking out being facilitated by the smooth surface of the flagged floor. After the smoke and soot had dispersed, a baking pan or tray containing the bread or other material to be baked would be inserted. Chimney damper and furnace door would then be closed, and the baking be carried out by radiant heat from the oven walls." [8]

Nothing that was found in the Duntocher oven gave any

---

[1] See below, p. 70, No. 1 ; p. 73, Nos. 5-10 ; p. 74, Nos. 2, 15-18 ; p. 77, No. 2 ; p. 80, No. 13 ; p. 81, Nos. 17, 19 ; p. 83, No. 26 ; p. 85, No. 28 ; p. 86, Nos. 41, 43 ; p. 87, No. 48.   [2] See below, p. 76, No. 7.

[3] Macdonald and Park, *The Roman Forts on the Bar Hill* (1906), pp. 56 ff.

[4] S. N. Miller, *The Roman Fort at Balmuildy* (1922), p. 40 and Pl. XIII B.

[5] *P.S.A.S.* xxx (1896), p. 101.

[6] *Arch. Æl.* (3), v (1909), pp. 246 ff. and Fig. 12.

[7] F. A. Bruton, *The Roman Forts at Castleshaw*, Second Interim Report (1911), pp. 20 ff. and Pl. 13.   [8] *P.S.A.S.* LXXVI (1942), p. 124.

definite clue to the nature of the food baked or roasted there. It may have been grain,[1] it may have been *buccellatum*, soldier's biscuit.[2]

There was evidence suggesting that the oven may have had two periods of use, or have been preceded by an earlier oven in a similar position. Heavily burned clay had spread over the turf-work in the north-east corner of the fort and had been later covered over by cobbling. The burned clay under the cobbling may have come from an oven contemporary with the turfwork, which was laid down early in the occupation of the fort.[3]

The Annexe and the Antonine Wall west of it

An area to the west of the fort was occupied by an annexe, in addition to the small military enclosure. That an annexe was envisaged from an early stage, at least from the time when the fort was being built, is proved by the absence of ditches on the west side of the fort.[4]

The annexe measured internally about 220 feet from east to west and about 150 feet from north to south. It had therefore an internal area almost twice that of the fort itself, and may be compared in this respect with the annexe at Rough Castle, whose internal area, in its first phase, was almost twice that of the fort.[5]

The Duntocher annexe was defended on its north side by the Antonine Wall and Ditch, and by the outer north ditch, on its south side by a rampart and three ditches which continued the line of the three south ditches of the fort, and on the west side by a rampart and one ditch. At what stage in the structural sequence at Duntocher the Antonine Wall was completed between the north-west corner of the fortlet and the north-west corner of the annexe is uncertain, but the building of this length of the Wall was

---

[1] *P.S.A.S.* LXXVI (1942), p. 125.

[2] Ammianus Marcellinus, XVII, 8 ; quoted in *P.S.A.S.* LXXIII (1939), p. 137 n.

[3] See above, p. 39.   [4] See above, p. 30.

[5] *P.S.A.S.* XXXIX (1905), pp. 450 ff.

probably either completed or its line known by the time that the west ditch of the annexe was dug, for the ditch stopped just short, by 2 feet, of the Antonine Wall.

Along the north front of the annexe, the Antonine Wall had, as elsewhere on Golden Hill, a breadth of 16 feet. The accompanying stretch of the Antonine Ditch was 20 feet wide, and that of the outer north ditch 14 feet wide.

At the north-west corner of the fortlet, or military enclosure, the Antonine Ditch lay 20 feet to the north of the Antonine Wall and the outer north ditch lay about 36 feet north of the Antonine Ditch.[1] Ninety feet further west, the distance between the two was 35 feet. At that point the Antonine Ditch swung northwards until at the north-west corner of the annexe it was 28 feet north of the Antonine Wall. The outer north ditch also inclined north-wards, maintaining a constant distance between itself and the Antonine Ditch, until, near the north-west corner of the annexe, it angled sharply south to join the Antonine Ditch. At the point of junction, the comb between the outer north ditch and the Antonine Ditch had been hardened with small stones and beaten clay. The Antonine Ditch then assumed an increased width of over 30 feet.

It would appear that the stretch of the Antonine Ditch on Golden Hill was dug from east to west, and that by the time it reached the north-west corner of the annexe, the outer north ditch was already being dug, or had been dug, and was ready, or expected, to join the Antonine Ditch and swell it to a greater breadth west of the annexe. This need not mean that the Antonine Ditch came late in the structural sequence, after the annexe was laid out. For the point at which the outer north ditch angled south to join the Antonine Ditch was a point where the western slope of the hill became rapidly steeper. This, rather than the presence of a completed annexe, may have brought the outer north ditch to an end, as it would also determine the western limit of a projected annexe.

[1] See above, p. 41.

Trenching on the north front of the annexe was much restricted. Such digging as was done, however, failed to reveal any sign of an entrance gap in either Antonine Wall or Ditch or outer north ditch.

West of the annexe, both Antonine Wall and Ditch turned slightly southwards to run down the hill towards the site of the modern bridge over the Duntocher Burn. Trenches cut on their line showed that the Antonine Wall base remained 16 feet wide,[1] while the Antonine Ditch increased in width to 36 feet. The interval between them was 26 feet.

A stretch of the Antonine Wall base here—about 18 feet in length—has been exposed for permanent exhibition in Golden Hill Park, under the auspices of Old Kilpatrick District Council. The stone base is in excellent preservation, with both rows of kerbstones quite intact. A stone culvert, about 1 foot wide, and 1 foot deep, bordered by large squared stones, runs across the base, its direction and slope suggesting that, unlike the culvert east of the fort,[2] it had drained water off to the south side of the Antonine Wall (Fig. 21).

Little, if anything, survived of the rampart which had once bounded the annexe on its south and west sides. The only material found which might have come from its super-structure was some clay lying over the stones of its base on the south side. There was too little of this, however, to justify an assertion that the annexe rampart had been of clay instead of turf.

It was only on the south front that the stone base of the rampart could be traced. The line of the rampart on the west front has now been largely usurped by one of the paths in the Park (Fig. 23). The south rampart base was 12 feet wide, and of markedly inferior build to the fort rampart base. Its stones were rough, unshaped

[1] From loose soil above the Antonine Wall base came two Samian fragments (form 37 and either 31 or 38), a mortarium rim, and two fragments of a jug (?). See below, p. 76, No. 8 ; p. 77, No. 3 ; p. 79, No. 6 ; p. 80, No. 12.
[2] See above, p. 11.

and jagged. In fact, on this south front, where the natural slope was so steep, the impression was received that the stones of the base had deliberately been allowed to assume upended positions in order to provide against the slipping of the rampart superstructure.[1] As it is, much of the base, as well as practically all the superstructure, has disappeared downhill. The filling of the innermost south ditch contained very many tumbled stones.

The poor preservation of the south rampart base of the annexe made it impossible to determine with certainty what sort of junction it had made with the rounded south-west corner of the fort. A few stones in a significant position, however, suggested that, as might be expected, the south rampart of the annexe had run straight on to join the south-west corner of the fort, thus maintaining a course parallel to that of the three south ditches. In loose soil at the probable point of junction was found a mortarium rim, stamped CICV.[2]

The three south ditches of the fort continued westwards to become the three south ditches of the annexe. The ground here had been much disturbed by the construction of children's swings, and of paths, and, further west, by the planting of a hedge. Still, there was space to cut trenches at sufficiently frequent intervals across the innermost south ditch to establish the fact that there had been no break in it for an entrance. It would, of course, have been strange had the annexe had a south entrance, when the fort had none.

The same trenches showed that the innermost ditch ran at a distance of 13-14 feet from the rampart. Moreover, this ditch, besides containing silt, in which were an amphora fragment and a fragment of an urn(?),[3] and above that later filling and tumbled stones, had large stones deliberately set on its inner edge at certain points, as if to harden its scarp. Such a feature has been noted elsewhere on this site, for

---

[1] From loose soil above the base came two Samian scraps. See below, p. 76, No. 10.

[2] See below, p. 79, No. 7.   [3] See below, p. 81, No. 15d.

example in the same ditch on the south front of the fort, and in the Antonine Ditch east of the fort.[1]

At only one point on the south front of the annexe was it possible to cut a trench across all three ditches (Fig. 23). Even here it was not possible to carry the trench down to the bottom of the ditches. In this trench, the ditches proved to have had the same dimensions as on the south front of the fort. The innermost ditch was 13 feet wide, the middle ditch was almost 14 feet wide and at least 6 feet deep, and the outermost ditch was 16 feet wide. The banks between each pair of ditches were 3-4 feet wide. In this same trench there was noted a hard gravel surface, 9 inches to 1 foot thick, covering the berm between the innermost ditch and the rampart base.

The south-west corner of the annexe is now the meeting place of two paths and a hedge (Fig. 23), but undismayed trenching did show that the three south ditches had been reduced to one at the corner, although it could not recover evidence for the manner in which the reduction took place. The three ditches might have combined into one, as at the south-east corner of the Antonine fortlet at Chew Green,[2] or else the middle ditch might have stopped, leaving the innermost and outermost ditches to combine into one, as happened, for example, at the south-east corner at Balmuildy.[3]

However that may be, one ditch only ran along the west side of the annexe at Duntocher.[4] It was half obliterated by a hedge planted in it, but one edge, the west edge, lay free of the hedge and was traced northwards. The ditch was apparently 14 feet wide, and was full of heavy grey silt. It came to a rounded end just 2 feet south of the Antonine Wall. At a point 54 feet south of the Antonine Wall, there was a gap in the ditch, 19 feet wide, through

---

[1] See above, pp. 11, 42.   [2] *Arch. Æl.* (4), XIV (1937), p. 141.
[3] S. N. Miller, *The Roman Fort at Balmuildy* (1922), p. 4 and Pl. LVIII.
[4] In loose soil outside the south-west corner were found two Samian fragments (form 33 and 18/31 or 31), a piece of an urn or bowl and two fragments of a bowl. See below, p. 75, No. 2 ; p. 76, No. 6 ; p. 81, No. 15*b* ; p. 85, No. 34.

E

which must have passed a road running west through the annexe from the west gate of the fort.

Time did not permit of any extensive exploration of the interior of the annexe. It was, however, noted that there was much cobbling outside the west gate of the fort, particularly over the filled-in south ditch of the fortlet, and to the south of it, and also behind the south rampart of the annexe. At one point behind the south rampart base there was found cobbling with ash and flecks of burned clay, possibly from a fire or oven.

A trench cut westwards from the fortlet, or military enclosure, revealed a slight hollow, about 5 feet across, a cluster of stones, and a pit or shallow depression, about $3\frac{1}{2}$ feet across and 1 foot deep, in which were scattered stones, the base of a Samian cup (form 27), stamped DRAV (CI ?), three amphoræ fragments showing traces of burning, a fragment of a bowl or lid, a scrap of a coarse ware vessel of hard red clay and another of soft red clay.[1] Further west were more stones and at least one rather ragged hole, about 1 foot across and 1 foot deep. North of the pit or shallow depression, there was, above the natural clay, a hard tramped surface, 4 inches thick, with charcoal scraps in it, and a shallow hole, less than 1 foot deep and 1 foot across, with charred wood in it, and a few stones round it. These remains, while demonstrating occupation of this area, were all either too disturbed or too indeterminate to be related to any definite structure.

From loose top soil at various points within the annexe there came other small finds. These included many scraps of wood, a fragment of flue tile with a diamond pattern scored on it, and forty small potsherds including four pieces of urns, and three bowl fragments found in the southern part of the annexe just outside the west fort rampart,[2] and scraps of wood, four pieces of a brick, a mortarium fragment and a bowl rim, found in the area west of the fortlet.[3]

[1] See below, p. 75, No. 1 ; p. 86, No. 47 ; p. 87, No. 52.
[2] See below, p. 74, No. 4 ; p. 87, No. 49.
[3] See below, p. 73, No. 1 ; p. 79, No. 6a ; p. 85, No. 29.

The Area north of the Outer North Ditch

When the outer north ditch was discovered, the possibility suggested itself that the level ground on the top of the hill—the most likely situation for a fort—had once been occupied by an Agricolan fort or fortlet, of which perhaps the outer north ditch had originally been the southern ditch. Trenching beyond the ditch, however, revealed no definite traces of recognisable structures, although at one point about 40 feet north of the ditch, there was burned clay and charcoal with which were a piece of an urn and a fragment of either a beaker base or a lid.[1] There had also been some disturbance of the ground, in the same area.

Also, trenches cut across the outer north ditch revealed, to the north of it, and at a distance varying from a few inches near its west end to 3 feet further east, a layer of turves about 1 foot thick and not more than 10 feet wide, at some points bedded in a hollow apparently made to receive it. In one section there were a few large stones under the turf layer, lying on the clay subsoil (Fig. 11). In another, nearer the west end of the ditch, the turf layer, here just north of the ditch, had stone pitching set in it, and in the edge of the ditch.

From the top of the dark turf layer came some tiny scraps of wood, eight pieces of daub, several of them with wattle-marks, and three pieces of the base of a Samian platter, with an indistinguishable potter's stamp.[2] Its poor quality indicates that it was of Antonine date. Immediately above the turf layer were three scraps of a mortarium rim.[3] All the material from this area, like that from the rest of the site, appears to be of Antonine date. There is nothing that can certainly be assigned to the late first century.

Nevertheless, the turf layer north of the outer north ditch calls for an explanation. It may simply be turf

---

[1] See below, p. 81, No. 17a ; p. 86, No. 46.　　[2] See below, p. 75, No. 3.
[3] See below, p. 77, No. 2.

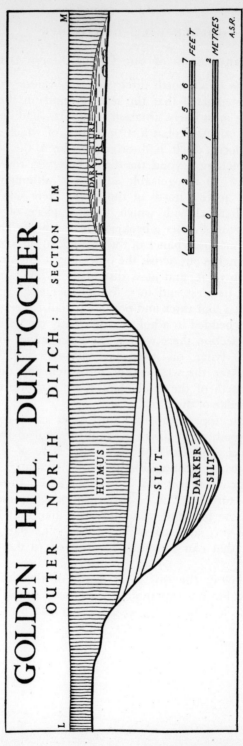

GOLDEN HILL, DUNTOCHER

OUTER NORTH DITCH : SECTION LM

FIG. 11. Section LM across outer north ditch

cut and removed before the outer north ditch was dug, and neatly disposed on the north side of it, as if perhaps to form a bed for the upcast mound, in the manner noted by Professor Richmond at Inchtuthil.[1] If so, however, it seems strange that at Duntocher the turf approached steadily closer to the outer north ditch as it ran westwards, that the turf, at some points, was bedded in a hollow apparently cut in the subsoil to receive it, and that, in one section at least, it was placed over large stones lying directly on the subsoil.

These features, small but undoubtedly present, make it unwise to discount altogether the possibility that the laid turf had once formed part of a turf rampart running along the south side of an enclosure lying to the north of the known Antonine works. If so, the fact that as the outer north ditch ran westwards it approached closer to the laid turf would suggest that a turf rampart may once have been accompanied by a ditch running parallel to it, or nearly so, and that the ditch had later been re-cut and given a slightly different course to become the outer north ditch. Unfortunately, digging on the line of the ditch was too restricted to make certain whether or not it had ever turned north at any point or points as if to enclose ground on top of the hill.

If there ever had been an enclosure surrounded by a turf rampart on top of Golden Hill, it may of course have been a proto-Antonine camp rather than an Agricolan fort.[2] A labour or building camp at Chew Green, for example, dating to the Antonine period,[3] was enclosed by an imposing rampart and ditch.

Whether, however, the top of the hill was ever the site of an independent structure, Agricolan or Antonine, cannot be decided without further excavation. That, at present, is out of the question.

---

[1] *J.R.S.* XLIII (1953), p. 104. [2] See below, pp. 89 ff.
[3] *Arch. Æl.* (4), XIV (1937), pp. 137 ff. See also below, pp. 90 f.

THE FINDS [1]

The harvest of finds was meagre in the extreme. Not a single piece of worked stone, or of shaped wood, or of leather or of bone, was recovered although scraps of charred wood were found at various points. There were, however, a few finds of metal, although they did not unfortunately include any coins.

Bronze (Fig. 12, Nos. 1-2)

1. A stud or dress-fastener with a rectangular head, $\frac{7}{8}$ in. by $\frac{3}{4}$ in., and a triangular looped stem, the surviving portion of which is 1 in. long. The base of the triangle is missing. The dress-fastener is too badly corroded for drastic cleaning, but it is possible to distinguish a narrow groove running round the rectangular plate, and slanting notches, each $\frac{1}{20}$ in. apart, cut along three of its edges. The fourth edge, without notches, is that nearest the loop.

From the oven in north-east sector of fort.

It is usually assumed that such objects were pushed through a slit or buttonhole in one side of a garment, and secured either by sewing or by some other means, while a loop attached to the other side of the garment was passed over the head of the fastener. At least eleven fasteners similar to the Duntocher example have been found in the native British hill fort at Traprain Law, East Lothian, besides many other fasteners or studs with petal-shaped or circular heads.[2] Four of them had a rectangular plate almost, but not quite as large as had the Duntocher fastener.[3] In one case, the rectangular plate had a groove round it, and also two diagonal grooves.[4] Three had triangular loops like the Duntocher example, and one had a pear-shaped loop.[5]

There were also seven dress-fasteners from Traprain with square heads or plates,[6] one of them enamelled.[7] The plates were on an average

---

[1] The finds have all been deposited in the Hunterian Museum, by permission of Old Kilpatrick District Council.

[2] A list of all the dress-fasteners found at Traprain is given in *P.S.A.S.* LVIII (1924), p. 264.

[3] *P.S.A.S.* XLIX (1915), p. 173 and Fig. 25, No. 8 ; LIV (1920), p. 79 and Fig. 11, No. 6 ; *ibidem*, p. 95 and Fig. 22, No. 8 ; and LVII (1923), p. 200 and Fig. 13, No. 10.

[4] *P.S.A.S.* XLIX (1915), p. 173 and Fig. 25, No. 8.

[5] *P.S.A.S.* LVII (1923), p. 200 and Fig. 13, No. 10.

[6] *P.S.A.S.* XLIX (1915), p. 173 and Fig. 25, No. 5 ; L (1916), p. 104 and Fig. 23, No. 16 ; LIV (1920), p. 67 and Fig. 7, Nos. 16-18 ; LV (1921), p. 186 and Fig. 21, No. 11 ; LVI (1922), p. 226 and Fig. 20, No. 6.

[7] *P.S.A.S.* XLIX (1915), p. 173 and Fig. 25, No. 5.

¾ in. square. One of these seven fasteners had a pear-shaped loop,[1] the others being triangular. None of the eleven square or rectangular fasteners from Traprain appear to have been notched round the edges.

That square-headed dress-fasteners, like those with petal-shaped heads,[2] were of native manufacture is shown by the discovery, at Traprain, of moulds for casting them.[3] The rectangular variety was probably produced by native craftsmen too. Circular fasteners, on the other hand, like those from sites as far apart as Newstead,[4] Chester [5] and the Saalburg,[6] were apparently of Roman origin.[7]

The square and rectangular fasteners found at Traprain came mainly from the lower levels, dating possibly from the late first century

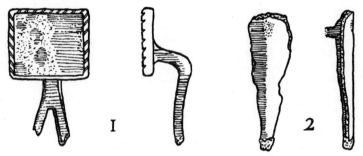

FIG. 12.   Objects of bronze.   Scale ¼

A.D., and certainly to the second century A.D. The Duntocher dress fastener is undoubtedly of Antonine date. Square and rectangular fasteners seem to have been recorded mainly from North Britain, although two examples were discovered at Wroxeter.[8]

2. Bronze attachment, possibly a terminal for a strap end, 1½ in. long by ½ in. broad. What survives of this much corroded object is a roughly triangular strip of bronze with a small knob at the foot. The surface is in two planes, meeting along the centre at an angle. On the

---

[1] *P.S.A.S.* L (1916), p. 104, and Fig. 23, No. 16.

[2] *P.S.A.S.* LVIII (1924), p. 264.

[3] *P.S.A.S.* L (1916), p. 124 and Fig. 37, No. 2.

[4] J. Curle, *The Fort of Newstead* (1911), p. 333 and Pl. LXXXIX, No. 22.

[5] In the Grosvenor Museum, Chester.

[6] L. Jacobi, *Das Römerkastell Saalburg* (1897), Pl. LIII, Nos. 12-13.

[7] Mr W. Dodds, of Hatfield College, Durham, who is at present engaged on a study of dress-fasteners is of the opinion that " the dress-fastener is a native idea that caught on with the Romans."

[8] *Research Report of the Society of Antiquaries*, I (1913), p. 29, Pl. X, 4, and IV (1916), p. 26, Pl. XVI, 15.

underside there is part of a projecting stem, possibly intended for fastening the bronze piece to a leather strap. An alternative but less likely possibility is that this fragment may have come from the lower part of a brooch, the projecting stem being part of the catch, although if so the catch must have been an open one with an unusual shape.

From loose soil in north-west sector of fort.

This bronze object bears some resemblance to a bronze strap terminal from Newstead,[1] and a bronze " attachment probably for a strap-end in harness " from Brecon,[2] which had five rivets for fastening it, probably to a leather strap. Not enough survives, however, of the Duntocher fragment to make certain what was its shape, when complete, and what was its purpose.

3. (Not ill.) Bronze pin, broken, in two pieces. The length of the surviving part is $3\frac{3}{4}$ in. and the diameter of its rounded stem is $\frac{3}{20}$ in. This pin has no features which would determine its purpose. It may not even be of Roman origin.

From loose soil above stone base at south-east corner of fort.

Iron

The objects of iron are too much corroded for cleaning. So little of the actual iron has survived that the objects would have disappeared entirely if cleaned.

1. Iron nail, apparently with a square head, about $\frac{5}{8}$ in. square, and a stem at least $2\frac{1}{4}$ in. long. This is a typical Roman nail, like those found in quantity at Balmuildy [3] and Newstead.[4]

From cluster of stones in north-west sector of fort.

2. Two pieces of iron which once formed part of a nail.

Near cluster of stones in north-west sector of fort.

3. Two fragments of iron nail, at least $2\frac{1}{4}$ in. long.

From loose soil above stone base at north-east corner of fort.

4. Six small iron nails, apparently with rounded heads, and stems averaging just over 1 in. in length. Nails as small as these have been recorded, for example, from Balmuildy [5] and Newstead.[6] They may well have been used as studs for a wooden door.

From loose soil over east fortlet base.

---

[1] J. Curle, *The Fort of Newstead* (1911), p. 301 and Pl. LXXVI, No. 9.

[2] R. E. M. Wheeler, *The Roman Fort near Brecon* (1926), p. 116 and Fig. 58, No. 15.

[3] S. N. Miller, *The Roman Fort at Balmuildy* (1922), p. 97 and Pl. LIV, Nos. 1-12.

[4] *Op. cit.*, p. 289 and Pl. LXVII, Nos. 21-34.

[5] *Op. cit.*, p. 97 and Pl. LIV, Nos. 5-8.

[6] J. Curle, *The Fort of Newstead* (1911), p. 289 and Pl. LXVII, No. 34.

5-10. Six iron fragments. Four are shapeless masses of rust. Another one seems to be part of a flat iron bar, of which 3¾ in. survives, ⅝ in. broad. The sixth is an iron ring about 1 in. in internal diameter, with an iron loop attached to it, and capable of being moved loosely on it. The loop now has only a single stem, which still survives to a length of 1 in., but it may originally have had a double stem. In that case, the object would bear a resemblance to the looped rings for attachment to wood-work from Newstead [1] and the Saalburg.[2]

From the oven.

11. Shapeless mass of rusted iron, about 4 in. long and 1 in. broad. This appears to be part of a straight length of an iron object, possibly a bolt, but its condition is too corroded for this to be certain.

From post-hole near north-east corner of fort.

12. Mass of material containing piece of iron pipe, of modern origin (see Appendix I).

From loose soil behind south rampart base of fort.

Daub

There were many pieces of daub. Eight of these, at least four of them showing wattle-marks, came from the dark turf layer north of the outer north ditch. From the oven came a piece of clay which possibly bears the impress of a post.

Bricks and Tiles

From a cluster of stones over the filled-in fortlet ditch in the north-west sector of the fort came a piece of soft clay with a red skin, possibly from a brick, and a piece of brick or tile, 6¼ in. by 5 in. by 1¼ in., of hard red clay. Also, from cobbling south of the extension to the north rampart base there came a piece of brick, 1⅞ in. thick. It was of hard red clay with a darker red coating on both surfaces. These three pieces of red tile or brick look different from most Roman tiles and may be post-Roman (see Appendix II). Certainly Roman, however, were the following bricks or tiles :

1. Square brick or tile, 6¾ in. square and at least 1¾ in. thick. This brick or tile probably came from a hypocaust pillar, but is slightly

---

[1] J. Curle, *The Fort of Newstead* (1911), p. 289 and Pl. LXVII, No. 12.
[2] L. Jacobi, *Das Römerkastell Saalburg* (1897), Pl. XLIII, Nos. 37 and 38.

smaller than usual. Even the smallest tiles used to form such a pillar were commonly at least 7 in. square. At Balmuildy, for example, where some hypocaust pillars in the Annexe Bath-house were found still standing to almost their full height, the smallest tiles were 7-8 in. square.[1] A square brick from the Bath-house at Mumrills was over 7 in. square.[2] From loose soil in annexe west of the fortlet.

2. Fragment of a larger brick or tile, probably square. The surviving part of the brick is $3\frac{3}{4}$ in. by 8 in., showing that the whole must have been at least 8 in. square, if it was square. It is 2 in. thick. This, too, was probably a hypocaust tile, or, if not, a floor tile.
From the filling-in in the oven area.

3. Fragment, $2\frac{5}{8}$ in. by $2\frac{1}{4}$ in., of flue tile, scored with diamond pattern.
From loose soil south of Antonine Wall in housing area.

4. Fragment, 2 in. by 2 in., of flue tile, scored with diamond pattern.
From loose soil in south part of annexe just outside west rampart of fort.

5. Fragment, $2\frac{1}{2}$ in. by 2 in., of flanged roofing-tile (*tegula*).
From loose soil south of Antonine Wall in housing area.

6. Fragment, 3 in. by 3 in., of semicylindrical roofing-tile (*imbrex*).
From loose soil south of Antonine Wall in housing area.

7. Fragment, 4 in. by $1\frac{3}{4}$ in., of semicylindrical roofing-tile (*imbrex*).
From loose soil over east fortlet base.

8. Curved fragment, 2 in. by $1\frac{1}{4}$ in., possibly from semicylindrical roofing-tile (*imbrex*).
From loose soil over stone base at north-east corner of fort.

9. Curved fragment, $3\frac{1}{2}$ in. by 2 in., possibly from semicylindrical roofing-tile (*imbrex*).
From loose soil over stone base at north-east corner of fort.

10. Curved fragment, 2 in. by $1\frac{1}{4}$ in., possibly from semicylindrical roofing-tile (*imbrex*).
From loose soil above south berm of fort.

11-20. Ten fragments of tiles, varying from 2 in. by $1\frac{1}{8}$ in. to 5 in. by $3\frac{1}{2}$ in. Four (11-14) came from loose soil south of the Antonine Wall in the housing area, four (15-18) from in and round the oven, and two (19-20) from clusters of stones in the north-west sector of the fort.

Pottery

Samian Ware.[3] There were fragments of not many more than a dozen vessels of Samian ware, not one of which

---

[1] S. N. Miller, *The Roman Fort at Balmuildy* (1922), p. 50.
[2] *P.S.A.S.* LXIII (1929), p. 546.
[3] The forms are according to Dragendorff.

need be dated to an earlier period than the second century.
There were no unmistakably Flavian pieces.

Plain Samian (*Fig.* 13, *Nos.* 1-7).   1. Lower part of cup (form 27) of
soft pink clay with dull glaze, stamped on the inside bottom DRAV(CI ?).
Diam. of base 1¾ in.

According to Felix Oswald, *Stamps on Terra Sigillata* (1931), pp.
111 and 383, *s.v. Draucus*, Draucus was a potter of Montans, and later
of Lezoux(?), working in the period Domitian-Trajan.   The form of his

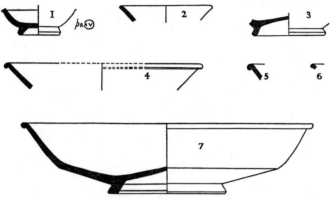

FIG. 13.   Plain Samian ware.   Scale ¼

stamp DRAVCI is recorded on a cup (form 27) at Amiens, and on cups
(form 33) at Corbridge and Newstead.   The Newstead stamp seems to
be exactly similar to the Duntocher stamp.   The cup on which it
occurred came from the inner ditch of the East Annexe, and is said to be
probably Gaulish, of the second century A.D.[1]

From pit or shallow depression in annexe.

2. Fragment of rim and side of cup (form 33), of soft red clay with
dull glaze, almost all flaked off.   Diam. 3⅛ in.

From loose soil outside south-west corner of annexe.

3. Three fragments of base of platter (form 18/31) of soft pink clay
with dull red-brown glaze, stamped on the inside bottom with a
indecipherable stamp.   Diam. 3 in.

From the dark turf layer north of the outer north ditch.

4. Fragment of rim and side of platter (form 18/31 or 31) of good
red clay with bright glossy red glaze.   Diam. 8½ in.

From loose soil behind east rampart base of fort.

---

[1] J. Curle, *The Fort of Newstead* (1911), p. 236.

5. Small fragment of rim of platter (form 18/31 or 31) of red clay with fairly good red glaze. Diam. uncertain.

From loose soil above north row of post-holes in west half of fortlet.

6. Scrap of rim, probably of platter (form 18/31 or 31) of soft red clay with dull glaze, almost all flaked off. Diam. uncertain.

From loose soil outside south-west corner of annexe.

7. Fragments forming the greater part of large platter (form 31 R), 12½ in. in diameter, of fairly hard red clay with good fairly bright glaze. It has a rouletted ring on the inside bottom, and in the centre a potter's stamp : C . . .

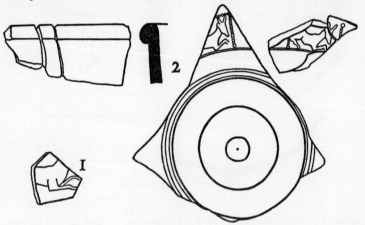

FIG. 14.   Decorated Samian ware.   Scale ½

Mr S. N. Miller has discussed platters of this type from Balmuildy, and noted that " it does not seem to have become at all common before the reign of Marcus." [1] At Duntocher, the position of the platter, found smashed on the floor of the oven, suggests that it belonged to the last days of the fort.

The following are not illustrated :

8. Fragment, possibly from the bottom of a large platter, or from a bowl (form 31 or 38 ?), of soft light pink clay with dull glaze.

From loose soil above Antonine Wall base west of annexe.

9. Fragment, possibly from the rim and side of a bowl, of good red clay with flat but good glaze.

From loose soil above south berm of fort.

10. Two scraps of Samian, possibly from a decorated bowl.

From loose soil above south rampart base of annexe.

---

[1] *The Roman Fort at Balmuildy* (1922), p. 64.

Decorated Samian (*Fig.* 14, *Nos.* 1-2). 1. Fragment of a decorated bowl (form 37) of soft red clay with rather dull glaze ; with part of a stag leaping r. (possibly Déch. 852 and Oswald 1720).

From loose soil over east fortlet base.

2. Six fragments of a decorated bowl (form 37) of bright red clay with rather dull glaze. Three fragments come from the rim (diam. about 7 in.), one from the base and lower part of the bowl, and two from the body. The decorated zone has been in panels, divided vertically and, in some cases at least, horizontally by rows of beads. At the bottom of two of the panels is a crouching deer (cf. Déch. 847 and Oswald 1704).

From the oven.

The following are not illustrated :

3. Fragment of a decorated bowl (form 37) of soft pink clay with dull glaze, showing a much rubbed ovolo.

From loose soil above Antonine Wall base west of annexe.

4. Fragment of a decorated bowl (form 37) of fairly soft pink clay with dull glaze, almost all flaked off. The surface is too badly rubbed for the decoration to be identified, but i⸱ appears to be in panels.

From the dump.

Coarse Ware. Several amphoræ fragments were found, most of them from the body of the vessels. One fragment of rim, however, and a piece from the body with an incised cross came from loose soil in the southern part of the fort, and a piece of base came from the oven.

Mortaria fragments came from over a dozen vessels (Fig. 15, Nos. 1-10).

1. Rim, showing spout, of mortarium of very hard white clay, with slight bead and rim thickened at edge. Internal diam. about 9 in. (Cf. *Old Kilpatrick*, Pl. XIX, No. 10.)

From the filling-in.

2. Three fragments of rim of mortarium, of very hard white clay, with rim similar to last, and possibly from same vessel. Internal diam. about 9 in.

From above the dark turf layer north of the outer north ditch.

3. Fragment of downcurving rim of mortarium of fairly hard white clay. Diam. uncertain. (Cf. *Old Kilpatrick*, Pl. XIX, No. 10.)

From loose soil outside north-east corner of fort.

3a. (Not ill.) Fragment of base of mortarium of hard white clay, well studded with grit. Diam. of base 4 in.

From burned material under cobbling of road through north gate of fort.

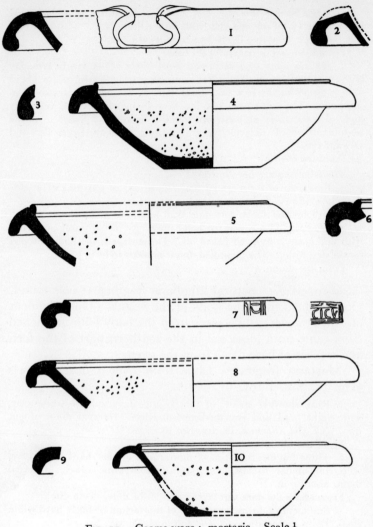

Fig. 15. Coarse ware : mortaria. Scale ¼

4. Fragments forming the greater part of a mortarium of rather soft buff clay, or light brown clay, with bead above level of short, hooked-over rim. Internal diam. 10 in. (Cf. *Balmuildy*, Pl. XLII, No. 32.)

From loose soil above south-west rampart base of fort.

5. Fragments of rim and side of mortarium of soft buff clay with bead above level of short, hooked-over rim. Internal diam, about 10 in. (Cf. *Balmuildy*, Pl. XLII, Nos. 32 or 36 and *Cadder*, Fig. 11, No. 9.)

Near clusters of stones in north-west sector of fort.

6. Fragment of thick rim of mortarium of fairly soft buff clay with bead about level with short, curving rim. Diam. uncertain. (Cf. *Balmuildy*, Pl. XLII, No. 25 and *Cadder*, Fig. 11, No. 11.)

From loose soil above Antonine Wall base west of annexe.

6a. (Not ill.) Fragment of base of mortarium of fairly hard buff clay.

From loose soil in annexe west of fortlet.

7. Fragment of rim of mortarium of soft red clay, with bead about level with hooked-over rim, stamped CICV. Internal diam. about 9 in. (Cf. *Balmuildy*, Pl. XLI, No. 22, and Pl. XL, No. 7 for stamp, and *Old Kilpatrick*, Pl. XIX, No. 20, and Pl. XVIII B, No. 3 for stamp, and *Bar Hill*, p. 70 for stamp.)

From loose soil outside south-west corner of fort.

8. Fragment of rim of mortarium of fairly hard red clay, without bead. Internal diam. about 12 in. (Cf. *Balmuildy*, Pl. XLI, No. 15.)

From loose soil in southern part of fort.

9. Fragment of outer edge of rim of mortarium of hard red clay. Diam. uncertain.

From loose soil behind south rampart base of fort.

10. Eight fragments of thin-walled mortarium of soft red clay, with bead almost level with curving rim. Internal diam. 7¾ in. (Cf. *Cadder*, Fig. 11, No. 7.)

From loose soil in southern part of fort.

The following are not illustrated :

10a. Two fragments of base of mortarium of soft red clay. Diam. of base 4 in.

From burned area north of stone platform behind south rampart base of fort.

10b. Two fragments of side of mortarium of fine pale pink clay.

From loose soil west of foundations in east sector of fort.

10c. Fragment of side of mortarium of red clay burned grey at the core with cream slip.

From loose soil south of Antonine Wall in housing area.

There were pieces of perhaps four jugs (Fig. 16, Nos. 11-14).

11. Fragment of " shelf " lip of jug of fine red clay. Diam. about

3 in. (Cf. the much larger jug, or pitcher, from *Balmuildy*, Pl. xxxix, No. 1.)

From filling-in at north-east corner of fort.

12. Two fragments of side of jug (?) of hard pink clay with two grooves on shoulder.

From loose soil above Antonine Wall base west of annexe.

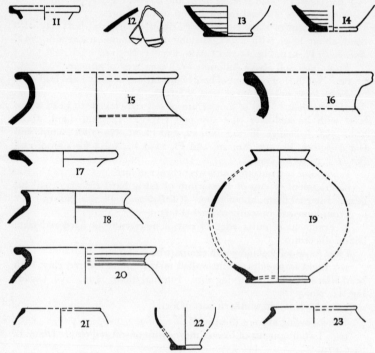

FIG. 16. Coarse ware : jugs, 11-14 ; urns, 15-17 ; ollæ, 18-20 ; beakers, 21-23. Scale ¼

13. Base of jug (?) of hard pinkish clay, showing traces of brownish slip, with moulded footstand and groove on outside bottom. Diam. 2 in.

From the oven.

14. Base of jug (?) of rather soft red clay washed with cream slip, with moulded footstand and groove on outside bottom. Diam. about 2 in.

From loose soil above south berm of fort.

At least half a dozen urns were represented (Fig. 16, Nos. 15-17).

15. Twelve fragments of neck, side and flat base of urn of red clay burned grey at the core, with outcurving rim and fairly long neck. Diam. of neck about 6 in. (Cf. *Balmuildy*, Pl. XLIV, No. 1.)
From burned material beside west wall of long narrow building.
15*a*. (Not ill.) Two fragments of side of urn (?) of red clay.
From loose soil west of foundations in east sector of fort.
15*b*. (Not ill.) Fragment of side of urn (?) or bowl (?) of soft pink clay.
From loose soil outside south-west corner of annexe.
15*c*. (Not ill.) Fragment of thick side of urn (?) of red clay.
From loose soil above cobbling in east half of fortlet.
15*d*. (Not. ill.) Fragment of thick side of urn (?) of red clay.
From silt in first south ditch of annexe.
16. Fragment of neck of urn of hard brown clay, smoothed, with offset at base of neck. Diam. of neck about 5 in. (Cf. *Balmuildy*, Pl. XLIV, Nos. 1 and 3.) [1]
From loose soil west of long narrow building.
17. Fragment of rim of urn of hard brown clay with dark grey slip, smoothed. Diam. 4½ in. (Cf. *Balmuildy*, Pl. XLIV, Nos. 1 and 3.)
From the oven.
17*a*. (Not ill.) Fragment of flat base of urn of coarse grey clay. Diam. uncertain.
From burned clay north of outer north ditch.

Fragments of ollæ were more numerous (Fig. 16, Nos. 18-20).

18. Three fragments of rim and side of olla of hard white clay with outcurving rim and shallow groove at base of it. Diam. 4½ in. An exactly similar rim, in the same clay, came from Balmuildy.[2]
From loose soil above cobbling in east half of fortlet.
19. Eight fragments of rim, side and base of olla or beaker of very hard brown clay with darker slip, smoothed, with fine, sharply everted rim (diam. 2 in.) and moulded footstand (diam. about 2¾ in.). The fineness of the rim, and the neat footstand suggest at first sight a first century date for this olla. It was, however, found in ash and other burned material near the oven together with other potsherds including many fragments of a fumed bowl. The rim resembles *Balmuildy*,

---

[1] An exactly similar urn fragment from Balmuildy is in the Hunterian Museum (F. 1922. 385).
[2] In the Hunterian Museum (F. 1922. 397-1).

F

Pl. xlv, No. 29 and *Old Kilpatrick*, Pl. xxi, No. 5, the latter possibly Flavian. The fabric and smoothed surface of the Duntocher fragments can be paralleled from other Antonine sites, for example from Balmuildy.[1]

20. Fragment of rim of olla of coarse grey clay with outcurving rim and slight grooves under it. Diam. about 6 in. (Cf. *Balmuildy*, Pl. xlv, Nos. 14-16, for shape, not fabric.)

From loose soil in west half of fortlet.

The following are not illustrated :

20*a*. Flat base of olla of grey clay. Diam. $3\frac{1}{2}$ in.
From top filling of narrow trench in east half of fortlet.

20*b*. Two fragments of flat base of olla of soft grey clay. Diam. uncertain.
From loose soil above cobbling in east half of fortlet.

20*c*. Fragment of flat base of olla of soft grey clay. Diam. about 3 in.
From burned area north of stone platform behind south rampart base of fort.

20*d*. Fragment of flat base of olla (?) of soft grey clay. Diam. uncertain.
Over, or in, cobbling in east half of fortlet.

20*e*. Fragment of side of olla of soft grey clay.
From top filling of narrow trench in east half of fortlet.

20*f*. Two fragments of flat base of olla of coarse fumed ware.[2] Diam. 3 in.
From cluster of stones in north-west sector of fort.

20*g*. Fragment of flat base of olla of coarse fumed ware. Diam. uncertain.
From post-hole near north-east corner of fort.

20*h*. Fragment of flat base of olla of coarse fumed ware. Diam. uncertain.
From below cobbling inside south gate of fortlet.

---

[1] In the Hunterian Museum (F. 1922. 403).

[2] On Antonine sites in Scotland, fumed ware divides itself sharply into two quite distinct types, each with its own characteristic rim sections. One, usually but not always black in colour, is coarse in texture. The other, usually but not always grey in colour, is fine in texture. A similar distinction has been noted by J. P. Gillam, when describing, for example, the group of late second century pottery from Corbridge (*Arch. Æl.* (4), xxviii (1950), pp. 177 ff.). The fine fumed ware appears to be on the whole later than the coarse fumed ware. The fumed ware from the Antonine Wall will be dealt with more fully in a projected publication describing the finds from the 1902-05 excavations at Bar Hill, which included a very large amount of pottery. The few fumed potsherds from Duntocher are too slender a peg on which to hang such a discussion.

20*j*. Fragment of side of olla of hard, fine fumed ware.
From loose soil in southern part of fort.

20*k*. Three fragments of side of olla of fine fumed ware.
From loose soil above cobbling in east half of fortlet.

20*l*. Two fragments of side of olla of fine fumed ware.
From loose soil above cobbling in east half of fortlet.

Less than half a dozen beakers were represented
(Fig. 16, Nos. 21-23).

21. Fragment of rim and side of fine beaker of very hard red clay,
with bead rim. Diam. about 3¼ in. (Cf. an example from Balmuildy,
F. 1922. 457, in the Hunterian Museum, and *Old Kilpatrick*, Pl. xxi,
No. 25.)
From loose soil south of Antonine Wall in housing area.

22. Six fragments of side and narrow base, probably of beaker, of
fairly hard red clay. Diam. of base 1¼ in.
From loose soil over east fortlet base.

22*a*. (Not ill.) Fragment of side of beaker, or small olla, of red clay
with red slip.
From loose soil south of Antonine Wall in housing area.

22*b*. (Not ill.) Fragment of side of beaker, or small olla, of red clay
with red slip.
From loose soil south of Antonine Wall in housing area.

23. Fragment of rim and side of beaker of fairly hard grey clay, with
bead rim. Diam. about 3½ in. (Cf. an example from Balmuildy,
F. 1922. 457, in the Hunterian Museum, and *Old Kilpatrick*, Pl. xxi, No.
25, for shape, not fabric.)
From loose soil above cobbling in east half of fortlet.

There were a few fragments of platters (Fig. 17, Nos.
24-26).

24. Fragment of side of large heavy platter of hard pink clay.
Diam. uncertain. (Cf. *Balmuildy*, Pl. xlviii, No. 23, and examples from
Bar Hill, F. 1936. 860-862, in the Hunterian Museum.)
From loose soil south of Antonine Wall in housing area.

25. Fragment of side of platter of fairly soft red clay. Diam.
about 12 in. (Cf. *Balmuildy*, Pl. xlviii, No. 23.)
From loose soil south of Antonine Wall in housing area.

26. Fragment of side of platter of fairly soft red clay. Diam.
uncertain.
From the oven.

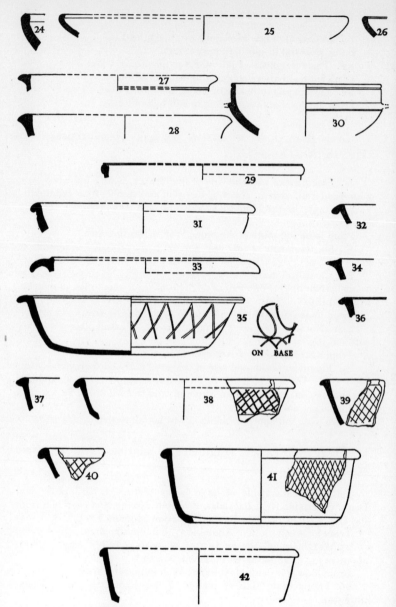

FIG. 17. Coarse ware ; platters, 24-26 ; bowls, 27-42. Scale ¼

Close on twenty bowls were represented (Fig. 17, Nos. 27-42).

27. Fragment of rim of heavy bowl of buff clay with roll rim slightly flattened on top. Internal diam. about 7½ in. (Cf. *Old Kilpatrick*, Pl. xxii, Nos. 11-12.)

From above cobbling inside south gate of fortlet.

28. Fragment of rim of heavy bowl of reddish buff clay with roll rim. Internal diam. about 8 in.

From the oven.

29. Fragment of rim of bowl of fine pink clay with roll rim having "shelf" inside. Internal diam. about 8½ in. This is an unusual rim, but resembles in some degree an early second century bowl rim from Corbridge.[1]

From loose soil in annexe west of fortlet.

30. Nine fragments of bowl of fine pink clay imitating the Samian form 37 or 44. Diam. 6¼ in. (Cf. *Balmuildy*, Pl. xlix, Nos. 12-15 and Pl. l, Nos. 21-22.)

From loose soil south of Antonine Wall in housing area.

31. Two fragments of heavy bowl of coarse pink clay with grey slip, with hooked rim. Internal diam. about 9 in. (Cf. *Balmuildy*, Pl. xlviii, No. 25.)

From post-hole near north-east corner of fort.

32. Fragment of rim of bowl of hard red clay, with flat, downbent rim. Diam. uncertain, probably 8-9 in. (Cf. *Old Kilpatrick*, Pl. xxii, No. 7.)

Near cluster of stones in north-west sector of fort.

33. Fragment of rim of mortarium-like bowl of soft red clay. Internal diam. about 8 in. (Cf. *Old Kilpatrick*, Pl. xxii, Nos. 25 and 26.)

From loose soil above south berm of fort.

34. Two fragments of rim probably of mortarium-like bowl, of soft red clay. Diam. uncertain.

From loose soil outside south-west corner of annexe.

35. Twenty-three fragments of rim, side and base of bowl of coarse fumed ware with flat rim, no chamfer between side and base, large lattice pattern on body and loops on base. Internal diam. 8½ in. (Cf. *Balmuildy*, Pl. xlvii, No. 5.)

From loose soil in southern part of fort.

36. Fragment of rim of bowl of coarse fumed ware with flat rim. Diam. uncertain, probably 6-7 in. (Cf. *Balmuildy*, Pl. xlvii, No. 6.)

From burned material under cobbling of road through north gate of fort.

---

[1] *Arch. Æl.* (4), xxxi (1953), p. 231 and Fig. 11, No. 30.

36*a*. (Not ill.)   Fragment of side of bowl (?) of coarse fumed ware with large lattice pattern.
Near cluster of stones in north-west sector of fort.

37. Fragment of rim and side of bowl of fine fumed ware, burned red, with roll rim.   Diam. uncertain, probably about 9 in.   (Cf. *Balmuildy*, Pl. XLVII, No. 9.)
From loose soil above north end of long narrow building.

38. Four fragments of rim and side of bowl of fine fumed ware, with roll rim, chamfer between side and base, and fine lattice pattern on side.   Internal diam. about 9 in.   (Cf. *Balmuildy*, Pl. XLVII, No. 9.)
From loose soil west of stone foundations in east sector of fort.

39. Two fragments of rim and side of bowl of fine fumed ware, burned red, with roll rim and fine lattice pattern.   Diam. uncertain.
(Cf. *Balmuildy*, Pl. XLVII, No. 9.)
From loose soil south of post-holes east of long narrow building.

40. Two fragments of rim, side and base of bowl of fine fumed ware, with roll rim and fine lattice pattern.   Diam. uncertain, probably about 8 in.   (Cf. *Balmuildy*, Pl. XLVII, No. 11.)
From the filling-in.

41. Twelve fragments of rim, side and base of bowl of fine fumed ware, with roll rim, chamfer between side and base, and fine lattice pattern.   Internal diam. 8 in.   (Cf. *Balmuildy*, Pl. XLVII, No. 12.)
From the oven.

42. Two fragments of rim and side of bowl of fine fumed ware, burned red, with roll rim.   Internal diam. about 8 in.   (Cf. *Balmuildy*, Pl. XLVII, Nos. 10-12.)
From loose soil west of stone foundations in east sector of fort.

There were also a few miscellaneous vessels represented (Fig. 18, Nos. 43-48).

43. Four fragments of lid of fairly hard buff ware with small knob on top.   Diam. 5½ in.
From the oven.

44. Fragment of lid of brown clay.   Diam. uncertain.
From loose soil south of Antonine Wall in housing area.

45. Fragment of lid of hard red clay.   Diam. uncertain.
From loose soil south of Antonine Wall in housing area.

46. Fragment of lid (?) or possibly narrow base of wide beaker (?) of soft red clay.   Diam. 1¾ in.   (Cf. *Balmuildy*, Pl. XLVI, No. 15 for base of beaker and *Castledykes*, Pl. LV, No. 30 for lid.)
From burned clay north of outer north ditch.

47. Fragment of thick vessel, possibly a bowl, less possibly a lid, of red clay with cream slip, with groove round edge. Diam. about 9 in.

From pit or shallow depression in annexe.

48. Two fragments of pedestal vessel of hard red brown clay, possibly a lid, (Cf. *Balmuildy*, Pl. xxxix, No. 8), or a tazza, (Cf. *Balmuildy*, Pl. L, Nos. 23-25.)

From the oven.

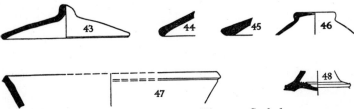

FIG. 18. Coarse ware : lids, etc. Scale ¼

The following are not illustrated :

49. Forty very small fragments, found in loose soil in annexe outside south-west rampart of fort, all seem to be of exactly the same red clay, but to come from different vessels. Two seem to be from the thick rim of an urn, one from a thinner urn rim, one from an urn base, and three from bowls. The remainder are indeterminate.

50. Fragment of soft red clay, from uncertain vessel.

From loose soil south of Antonine Wall in housing area.

51. Three scraps of red clay from uncertain vessels.

From loose soil over east fortlet base.

52. Two fragments of red clay, from uncertain vessels.

From pit or shallow depression in annexe.

SUMMARY AND CONCLUSIONS

THERE IS AS YET no sure evidence that Golden Hill was ever the site of one of the forts established by Agricola in A.D. 81 (or A.D. 80), on the Forth-Clyde isthmus.[1] No structural remains and no small finds were recovered which could with certainty be dated to the late first century A.D.

Still, there persists the possibility, even perhaps the probability, that the level ground on top of the hill, with its wide view in all directions, was selected by Agricola as a suitable site for a fort. Reluctance to abandon this possibility is of course supported by the consideration that of the ten Antonine Wall forts so far excavated almost all have yielded evidence for a first century occupation. Remains of Agricolan forts themselves have actually been found under the Antonine Wall forts at Mumrills,[2] Croy Hill[3] and Bar Hill,[4] and possibly at Old Kilpatrick,[5] at Rough Castle[6] and at Cadder,[7] while late first century pottery has been recovered from the Antonine Wall fort at Castlecary,[8] as well as from Rough Castle[9] and Cadder.[10] An eighth fort, Westerwood,[11] has also given a hint of an Agricolan occupation.

Only at Balmuildy[12] and at Duntocher is evidence for an Agricolan occupation so far completely lacking. The late Mr S. N. Miller, however, suggested the possibility that at Balmuildy an Agricolan fort may have occupied

---

[1] Tacitus, *Agricola*, c. 23.
[2] *P.S.A.S.* LXIII (1929), pp. 400 ff.
[3] *P.S.A.S.* LXVI (1932), pp. 262 ff.
[4] Macdonald and Park, *The Roman Forts on the Bar Hill* (1906), pp. 11 ff.
[5] S. N. Miller, *The Roman Fort at Old Kilpatrick* (1928), pp. 51 ff.
[6] *P.S.A.S.* LXVII (1933), pp. 262 ff.
[7] John Clarke, *The Roman Fort at Cadder* (1933), pp. 84 ff.
[8] *R.W.*, pp. 250 ff.
[9] *R.W.*, p. 238.   [10] *Loc. cit.*
[11] *P.S.A.S.* LXVII (1933), pp. 283 f.
[12] S. N. Miller, *The Roman Fort at Balmuildy* (1922), p. 103.

a slightly different position from the Antonine fort.[1] Duntocher must be left meantime with the hope that the beguiling level ground on top of the hill may one day be released for further exploration.

Should such a time ever come, there would have to be taken into account the laid turf on the north edge of the outer north ditch, and the burned clay and charcoal noted about 40 feet north of the ditch, together with some disturbance of the ground, unfortunately of a nature and date as yet undetermined, in the same area. The turf may simply have been placed on the outer edge of the outer north ditch when it was first cut, possibly as bedding for an upcast mound, which may or may not have had obstacles of some kind set in it (some scraps of wood were found on the turf). On the other hand, the turf may represent the remains of a rampart, originally erected along the south side of an enclosure on top of the hill and accompanied to south by a ditch, which was later given a very slightly different alignment to become the " outer north ditch." The pre-existence of an enclosure of some kind on top of the hill and the survival of an earlier ditch in a usable form would undoubtedly offer an attractive explanation for the doubling of the Antonine Ditch and for the fact that the outer north ditch did not maintain an exactly parallel course to the Antonine Ditch for the whole of its length.

An earlier enclosure, if such there were, may not of course have been of Agricolan origin, but an Antonine camp for troops engaged in building work of some kind. It is, as Mr John Clarke remarked twenty years ago, " rather strange that no trace of the encampments of the legionary vexillationes who built the Wall have yet been found. Such encampments there must have been." [2] The only possible remains of such encampments so far noted are at Cadder itself,[3] at a site north-east of Balmuildy, and at Kinglass

---

[1] *The Roman Occupation of South-Western Scotland* (1952), p. 214 n.
[2] John Clarke, *The Roman Fort at Cadder* (1933), p. 86.
[3] *Ibidem.*

Park south of Bo'ness, at Little Kerse east of Polmont, at Milnquarter, and at Tollpark, south-west of Castlecary, where the crop-marks of ditches have been observed from the air by Dr St Joseph.[1] At Duntocher, too, it may be that in the Antonine period a working squad occupied the site first, and built a temporary enclosure for itself.

However that may be, the earliest permanent Antonine structure identified on the site was a fortlet, set on the most commanding position on the hill, at the south-western extremity of the plateau. At first it was an isolated structure, surrounded on all four sides by a ditch, as well as by a turf rampart set on a stone foundation.

When it stood alone, the fortlet had had its main entrance to north, and another, exactly opposite, to south. To the latter probably belonged two rows of three large post-holes, plainly intended to hold posts supporting a massive gate structure or even a small tower. The north (main) gate must have been of no less massive character.

To the occupation of the fortlet as an isolated structure may have belonged the two stretches of narrow trench, lying 18 feet from the east and west ramparts of the fort respectively, and later covered with cobbling. These trenches, sharply defined and filled with burned clay and flecks of charred wood, had most likely held bed plates for a timber-framed building with wattle and daub filling. The two trenches, however, were not of equal lengths. Rather than having belonged to the same building (which in that case would have stood right in the centre of the fortlet opposite the north and south gates—an inconvenient situation) they may have belonged to two different buildings, one on either side of the central roadway. If so, no traces of the other sides of these buildings were identified, unless perhaps they were represented by the black-filled post-holes.[2]

It is, on the other hand, just possible that none of the

[1] *J.R.S.* XLI (1951), p. 62, and XLV (1955), p. 86.
[2] See also below, p. 101.

remains noted within the fortlet, neither trenches nor post-holes, belonged to the fortlet in its independent form. In that case, the remains of the fortlet buildings may either still await discovery or may never have been completed. Yet the fortlet defences and entrances were certainly completed, and it seems likely that some at least of the internal buildings would have been completed too. Either, then, traces of these have not been found, or they must be represented by the two narrow trenches, and possibly the black-filled post-holes, the earliest structural remains yet identified in the fortlet.

No potsherds or other finds were recovered from the fortlet ditch in any of the twenty or more sections cut across it. Nor did any finds come out of the narrow trenches, although on top of the more easterly one there lay a frag-ment of one olla, and the base of another. There was no object which could, either with certainty or even probability, be assigned to the occupation of the fortlet as an independent structure. All the finds indeed from the area of the fortlet, as from the site generally, can be paralleled from other Antonine sites and appear to be of Antonine date. There is not a scrap of evidence for an occupation of the fortlet earlier than the Antonine period. On the contrary, the fact that its ditch contained no silt under the deliberate filling shows that, when it was levelled to allow the Antonine fort to be built, this took place not after a period of abandon-ment, but during the continuous occupation of the site.

Although of Antonine date, the fortlet inevitably invites comparison with a milecastle on the Turf Wall sector of Hadrian's Wall, for example, that at High House.[1] What, if any, is the significance of this resemblance between the Duntocher fortlet and a Turf Wall milecastle,[2] and what was the purpose of the fortlet is difficult to say in view of the fact that it is so far the only recorded example of a fortlet on the Antonine Wall. The " guard-house " between

[1] *Trans. Cumb. and West. A.S.*, n.s. xxxv (1935), pp. 220 ff.
[2] See also below, p. 108.

Rough Castle and Falkirk [1] and the two recently discovered
enclosures attached to the Antonine Wall in Wilderness
Plantation, east of Balmuildy, and at Glasgow Bridge, west
of Kirkintilloch,[2] were all much larger, measuring 100 feet
square or more.   It is therefore not known whether the
Duntocher fortlet formed part of a scheme involving the
use of other fortlets and should be explained on these
terms, or whether it was an isolated phenomenon.   If the
latter, it may be, to quote a letter on the subject from
the late Mr S. N. Miller, that " the fortlet was designed to
become ultimately a permanent part of the general lay-
out without any ditch, but in the initial phase it would be
useful, on that dangerous site, to house and protect the men
building the fort, or some of them, or their tools and stores,
with a guard, and so they built it right away and gave it a
defensive character, surrounding it with a ditch.   Then
when the fort was ready for occupation, they filled in the
ditch, and the little fortlet assumed the permanent function
for which it was intended.   Something of the same kind
may have happened at Milton, with the south enclosure
or annexe, where the north rampart, like the fortlet ditch
at Duntocher, may have served a temporary purpose." [3]

It is true that the fortlet did in time become part of a
larger fortified work, and it is true, to judge from the fact
that its north corners were squared externally, while its
south corners were probably rounded, that its builders
most likely anticipated from the first that it would do so.
Yet the position of the fortlet on the best site on the hill,
the carefully laid rampart base with its two rows of very
massive kerb-stones, and neatly fitted small stones between
them, the ditch with its regular dimensions and its scrupu-
lously constant distance from the rampart base, and the two
gates, almost certainly of massive character, all suggest
that the builders attached great importance to the immediate

[1] *R.W.*, p. 344.
[2] *J.R.S.*, XLI (1951), p. 61, and XLV (1955), p. 86.
[3] *Trans. Dumfriesshire and Galloway Nat. Hist. and Ant. Soc.*, XXVII (1950),
pp. 197 f.

purpose of the fortlet as an isolated structure, even more importance perhaps than they attached to its possible future use as an adjunct to a larger work. In its own right, it served, or was meant to serve, an important purpose of some kind.

It may be that at Duntocher (and perhaps at other places) it was thought advisable to establish a watch post at a key point on the line of the Wall before the Wall was built. Certainly this sector of the Wall was extremely vulnerable to an enemy swooping down from the north,[1] and certainly the position of the fortlet, on the most commanding spot on Golden Hill, made it an ideal watch post. A unit stationed there would have a wide outlook in every direction, particularly if, as seems possible, there were gate-towers to provide still higher viewpoints, from which too signals could have been sent.

Mr John Clarke has indeed suggested to me " that the fortlet may have belonged to an early phase of the Wall-project when the terminal fort at Old Kilpatrick stood in isolation and the Wall, proceeding by sections from the east,[2] was still some distance off. If indeed there was an early phase, perhaps a whole winter, when Old Kilpatrick stood in isolation, an elementary military necessity would be the institution of patrols from Old Kilpatrick as a base along the dangerous ground facing the Kilpatrick Hills in such close proximity.[3] The fortlet can best be explained as a unit of such a patrol system, and it would not be surprising if a similar structure were in time to be found at Castlehill. The fortlet, it is true, differed from the fort at Old Kilpatrick in that it assumed the arrival of the Wall (or some other work) by the square build of its northern front. This is not surprising, however, for its construction must have come after the terminal fort had established a

[1] Cf. S. N. Miller, *The Roman Fort at Balmuildy* (1922), p. 2, and *The Roman Occupation of South-Western Scotland* (1952), pp. 214 ff.

[2] See below, pp. 96 ff.

[3] For a similar suggestion, see S. N. Miller, *The Roman Occupation of South-Western Scotland* (1952), p. 215.

general control of the area and the second phase, the actual construction of the Wall, had begun in sections from the east."

Whatever its original purpose, the question inevitably suggests itself whether the fortlet was ever intended to take the place of a fort attached to the Antonine Wall. This would be an abnormality, but the squared north corners do suggest that it was a junction with the Antonine Wall rather than absorption by a larger fort that was expected. Indeed, the re-use of the fortlet as an adjunct to a fort meant that the east fortlet rampart had, as it were, to be turned inside out. For if its inner slope had been much less steep than its outer slope, as one would expect, this would have to be adjusted in some way when the fort was added.

Whether or not the fortlet was originally intended to take the place of a fort or to serve another purpose, temporary but nonetheless important, it was in a short space of time superseded by, or rather made an appendage of, a fort. The fort was in fact deliberately laid out in a position which enabled its builders to retain the fortlet in use as an adjunct to the fort. Their decision to use the fortlet in this way gave the fort a somewhat awkward situation, so that it lay partly down the southern slope of the hill.

By the time the fort was added to the fortlet, the Antonine Wall had not been built, although the Antonine Ditch may have been dug.[1] The structural sequence at Duntocher —fortlet, fort, Antonine Wall—gives strong support to the view that the Antonine Wall was built from east to west, rather than from west to east. (The fact that, on Golden Hill, the length of the Antonine Wall which was brought up to the east rampart of the fort was clearly built from the east, does not of itself prove that the whole of the Antonine Wall was built from east to west. It merely proves that one short stretch of the Antonine Wall on the east side of the fort on Golden Hill was erected by men who chose, or who were instructed, to work from east to west.)

[1] See above, pp. 40, 47, and below, p. 100.

The view that the Wall was built from east to west was, by Sir George Macdonald, based on the evidence of the distance slabs.[1] He pointed out that on the distance slabs there is a change in the unit of measurement at Castlehill, 4 miles from the west end of the Wall. The distance slabs found in the 4-mile sector between Castlehill and Old Kilpatrick record the completion of short lengths of the Wall, each measured in feet, while the distance slabs found to the east of Castlehill, between Castlehill and the Forth, record the completion of long stretches, each measured in Roman paces.

Sir George Macdonald explained the change in the unit of measurement at Castlehill by supposing that the building of the Antonine Wall was begun from the east, and was expected to be completed in nine lengths or sectors, each of which was assigned to a particular working squad. The working squad assigned to the fifth length, however, found itself confronted on Croy Hill with the task of cutting the Antonine Ditch through solid rock, and lagged far behind the other squads. By the time the ensuing confusion was straightened out, there was an odd sector, from Castlehill to the Clyde, left over at the western end of the Wall. This, Sir George Macdonald suggested, was subdivided into six short lengths, built by six separate working squads, two drawn from each of the three legions engaged in the construction of the Wall.

There is no doubt that the 4-mile sector from Castlehill to the Clyde was built in six separate lengths, each measured in feet, for the completion of which the Second, the Sixth and the Twentieth Legions supplied two working squads each. Distance slabs from all six lengths survive to prove that. There is not, however, a complete enough series of distance slabs surviving from the 33-mile long stretch of the Antonine Wall from Castlehill eastwards to the Forth to prove how that part of the work was organised, and to suggest why the change in the unit of measurement from

[1] *J.R.S.* xi (1921), pp. 1 ff., and *R.W.*, pp. 394 ff.

paces to feet, or from feet to paces, became advisable. Mr S. N. Miller has indeed put forward the theory that the reason why, west of Castlehill, the legionary working squads were allotted short instead of long stretches, and so were in closer touch with one another, was simply because " here they were working under the immediate threat of ' assaults and interruptions' from the Kilpatrick Hills. It was a sector which they would be anxious to finish off as quickly as possible and where they would have good reason to take special precautions for their security." [1]

Another, perhaps more weighty, argument in favour of the view that the Wall was built from east to west is provided by the forts so far excavated on its line, and is now strongly reinforced by the structural sequence at Duntocher. Of the forts in the eastern and central sectors of the Wall, Mumrills, Rough Castle, Westerwood, Croy Hill and Cadder had their ramparts completed either after, or at the same time as, the Wall was built. The Wall itself formed the north rampart of each of these five forts.

At Mumrills, the Antonine Wall builders and the fort builders were apparently working in co-ordination.[2] At Rough Castle,[3] Westerwood [4] and Croy Hill [5] the Antonine Wall base had been laid down first and the east and west fort rampart bases had either butted up against the Wall base or even slightly overlapped it. At Cadder [6] too the Wall base had apparently been laid before the fort rampart bases but with the needs of the fort in view. Here too, as at Mumrills, Wall and fort builders were probably at work together. At the other known forts east of Cadder—Castlecary and Bar Hill—evidence for or against the Antonine Wall having been built first was not forthcoming. The fort at Castlecary had been girt by a stone wall on all four sides,

---

[1] *The Roman Occupation of South-Western Scotland* (1952), p. 216.

[2] *P.S.A.S.* LXIII (1929), pp. 406 ff., and Plan ; *R.W.*, pp. 195 ff.

[3] *P.S.A.S.* XXXIX (1905), pp. 451 ff. ; *R.W.*, p. 220.

[4] *P.S.A.S.* LXVII (1933), p. 280 ; *R.W.*, p. 255.

[5] *P.S.A.S.* LXVI (1932), p. 247 ; *R.W.*, p. 261.

[6] John Clarke, *The Roman Fort at Cadder* (1933), pp. 10 ff. ; *R.W.*, pp. 303 ff.

and had not used the turf rampart of the Antonine Wall as its northern defence.[1] The Antonine fort on the Bar Hill lay, detached, a short distance south of the Antonine Wall so that it is impossible to say whether it was built before or after it.[2]

The excavated forts west of Cadder on the other hand were all built before the Antonine Wall was completed. The fort at Balmuildy, apparently guarding a crossing of the River Kelvin, was, like Castlecary, defended by a stone wall. The builders had not only completed the stone wall on all four sides of the fort, but had also built projecting wings out from its north-east and north-west corners before the Wall builders arrived.[3] The terminal fort on the west at Old Kilpatrick had had all four corners rounded, and must have stood alone for a time before the Wall was built.[4] "As a preliminary to the building of the Wall a site was occupied commanding the waterway of the Clyde." [5]

At Duntocher the Antonine Wall was preceded not only by a fort, but also by a fortlet, both of Antonine date. Duntocher lies only 2 miles from the western end of the Antonine Wall at Old Kilpatrick. If the building of the Wall had proceeded from Old Kilpatrick eastwards, there would not have been time to build a fortlet, perhaps to occupy it for some period, and then to add a fort to it, before the Wall arrived. There would have been time, if the Wall had been built from the Forth westwards. On present evidence, then, it seems almost certain that the Antonine Wall was begun from the east and that some sites at least in the western sector were held by forts (or, at

---

[1] *P.S.A.S.* xxxvii (1903), pp. 289 ff. ; *R.W.*, p. 243.

[2] Macdonald and Park, *The Roman Forts on the Bar Hill* (1906), pp. 15 ff. ; *R.W.*, p. 273.

[3] S. N. Miller, *The Roman Fort at Balmuildy* (1922), pp. 6 ff ; *R.W.*, pp. 162 ff., 313 ff.

[4] S. N. Miller, *The Roman Fort at Old Kilpatrick* (1928), pp. 55 ff. ; *P.S.A.S.* xvii (1932), pp. 226 ff.

[5] *Loc. cit.*, p. 55.

Duntocher, by a fortlet and then by a fort) before the Wall arrived.

When completed, the fort at Duntocher had an internal area of about half an acre, and was defended by a turf rampart on a stone base, and by three ditches on its east and south sides. It had three gates, in its east, west and north sides, and the north gate must surely have had a gate-tower providing a view over the level ground to north. The north gate (and gate-tower?) of the fortlet may then have been disused or else supplanted by a less massive gate. In the north-east corner of the fort at least there seems to have been an *ascensus* leading to the rampart walk.

The Antonine Wall joined the east fort rampart 10 feet south of the north-east corner, and the Military Way, when completed, skirted the southern defences and sent off a branch to the east gateway. From the west gateway a road ran out westwards, sending off a branch through the south gate of the former fortlet, now a military enclosure attached to the fort. The massive south gate first planned for the fortlet probably remained in use during the first period in the occupation of the fort. There may also have been a direct entry from the north-west sector of the fort into the military enclosure.

To the west of the fort was an annexe defended on south and west sides by a rampart of less careful construction than the fort rampart, and on the north side by the Antonine Wall. The addition of an annexe to the fort must have been planned as early as the fort itself for there had never been any ditches on the west side of the fort, and the three south fort ditches continued in a straight line along the south side of the annexe to the south-west corner, where they were reduced to one. By the time the digging of the annexe ditches was completed, the stretch of the Antonine Wall along the north front of the annexe was probably either built or its approximate line was known, for the west annexe ditch stopped short by 2 feet of the line taken by the Wall.

If so, it is likely that the stretch of the Wall, or at least the Wall base, east of the fort had also been completed. The laying out of the fort and the annexe, and the building of the stretches of the Antonine Wall east and west of the fort were probably not separated by any great lapse of time.

The entire north fronts of the fort, military enclosure and annexe were covered by the Antonine Ditch and by an outer north ditch which may possibly have re-used, for part of its length, a pre-existing ditch running along the south side of an enclosure to the north. The completion of the Antonine Ditch may have come fairly early in the structural sequence, for the divergence between the north front of the fort and that of the fortlet seems best explained on the grounds that the Ditch had been laid out with the north rampart of the fortlet in view, and that the north rampart of the fort had later been set parallel to the Ditch.[1] By the time the Ditch reached the north-west corner of the annexe, the outer north ditch, it seems, was being dug or had been dug, and was expected to join the Antonine Ditch and increase its width.

If the Ditch was dug before the fort was built, this would no doubt explain why there was no break for a causeway in the Ditch opposite the north gate of the fort. Since the fortlet certainly came before the Ditch, the Ditch diggers may rather have allowed for a causeway opposite the fortlet, and this may have been dug away later when the fort was built. Or, perhaps, the outer north ditch was already in existence, to discourage, by an unbroken line, the provision of a causeway in the Antonine Ditch.

The doubling of the Antonine Ditch (on the north front of a fort at least) has not been noted elsewhere on the Antonine Wall. At Duntocher it appears to represent an attempt to break up the level ground to the north of a fort the choice of whose position had apparently been influenced by the decision to incorporate and re-use an earlier fortlet. The north edge of the outer north ditch may have had a

---

[1] See above, p. 47.

carefully disposed upcast mound, possibly with obstacles of some sort planted on it.

Apart from the doubling of the Antonine Ditch, the completed plan of the Antonine works at Duntocher bears a close resemblance to that at Rough Castle, the next smallest fort on the Wall. There, an annexe lay to the east of the fort, with an area almost twice that of the fort itself, and within this annexe, just outside the east gate of the fort, there was a small military enclosure. At Rough Castle, however, no evidence was recovered which suggested that the small enclosure had ever been an independent structure, like the Duntocher fortlet. In its earliest form, it had been delimited on its two free-standing sides (east and south) by a ditch only, to which was later added a palisade, which was still later replaced by an earthen mound. Sir George Macdonald suggested that it may first have served as a barrack yard, and later as a storage place.[1]

At Duntocher, the enclosure had at first apparently contained two wooden buildings, set one on either side of the central road, to which probably belonged the black-filled post-holes, and possibly the two narrow trenches, if these did not date only to the occupation of the fortlet. These had all been dug down deep into the subsoil and were later covered by cobbling. It is of course quite possible that buildings erected when the fortlet was an independent structure were simply re-used as they stood, as the south gate probably was, when the fort was added. If so, narrow trenches and black-filled post-holes must have been in use together, both during the fortlet period and during the first occupation of the military enclosure. However that may be, there were apparently two wooden buildings in the enclosure during its first occupation as an adjunct to the fort. These may have been barrack blocks. If so, together they would probably hold about 50 men.

Even so small an addition to the living accommodation

---

[1] *P.S.A.S.* LXVII (1933), pp. 254 ff.

on the site would have been welcome when the fort itself
was so small. To its initial occupation belonged the small
squarish building (probably stone-built), which stood in the
position of, and may even have served the purpose of, the
main administrative building. Room would also have to be
found for officers' quarters, and for at least a granary, if
not for other stores or workshops. (The bath building lay
outside the fort to the west.[1]) To one or other of such
buildings possibly belonged stone foundations near the
east rampart and south of the east gate, tumbled stones in
the north-west sector of the fort, and gulleys or trenches
between the small central building and the south rampart.
One of these last at least dated to an early period in the
occupation of the fort, for it was covered by a later building,
and by made-up soil.

There would thus remain within the fort little more than
half its area for barracks. One of these apparently lay
immediately east of the small central building and was
represented by black-filled post-holes dug down deep into
the subsoil, like those in the enclosure. Another barrack
block at least probably lay in the north-east sector of the
fort, where there seems to have been an oven.[2] Ovens in
forts appear usually to have been placed in relation to
barracks.[3]

There is, unfortunately, insufficient information available about the internal arrangements of small forts in
Britain to justify an attempt to work out the barrack plan
at Duntocher, and estimate the strength of its garrison.
In size the fort resembles, for example, the small Hadrianic
fort at Castleshaw which had an area of $\frac{5}{8}$ acre, and the
small Trajanic forts at Throp and Haltwhistle, each of
which had an internal area of about $\frac{2}{3}$ acre. Only one of
the internal buildings of the small fort at Castleshaw was
examined. It was a hypocausted structure, 15 feet square.[4]

[1] See above, p. 4.   [2] See above, p. 61.
[3] Cf. Professor I. A. Richmond, in *P.S.A.S.* LXXIII (1939), p. 138.
[4] F. G. Bruton, *The Roman Forts at Castleshaw*, Second Interim Report
(1911), p. 19.

The fort at Haltwhistle contained stone buildings of very irregular shape and disposition, and indefinite purpose.[1] " The arrangement of the buildings is quite different from that of the larger forts, and lacks the familiar regularity and balance." [2] Buildings at Throp had probably been of timber. Their presence was attested only by areas of flagging and stone pitching, and by hearths.[3] The considerably larger Antonine fort at Cappuck " was equipped with principal buildings of stone, but had no headquarters of normal type. The barrack blocks were perhaps of timber." [4]

Fragmentary as are the plans of these forts, they do suffice to show that they were provided with principal buildings of some kind as well as with barracks, and were not simply fortlets like, for example, the fortlet at Cardurnock on the Cumberland coast, with living accommodation for patrol garrisons only.[5] At Duntocher too, only part of the internal area was available for living accommodation. It may be suggested, tentatively, that fort (and enclosure) may have held two centuries. This, however, can only be a guess.

The Duntocher annexe has not been sufficiently examined to warrant any discussion of its use. Such evidence of occupation as was recovered did not indicate whether it was of a civilian or of a military character. The use of an annexe for purely military purposes would be unusual, but on the other hand the provision of an annexe at Duntocher was planned from the time the fort was being built. Apart from that, there is at present no ground for considering the possibility that the annexe, as well as the military enclosure, had ever held part of the garrison force on Golden Hill.

---

[1] *Arch. Æl.* (3), v (1909), pp. 220 ff. ;   *Trans. Cumb. and West. A.S.*, n.s. xiii (1913), pp. 379 ff.

[2] *Arch Æl.* (3), v (1909), p. 250.

[3] *Trans. Cumb. and West. A.S.*, n.s. xiii (1913), pp. 363 ff., and p. 372.

[4] *P.S.A.S.* lxxxv (1951), p. 145.

[5] *Trans. Cumb. and West. A.S.*, n.s. xlvii (1947), pp. 85 ff.

That being so, the accommodation for military purposes, and the garrison at Duntocher, were the smallest, so far as is known, in any fort on the line of the Antonine Wall.   The

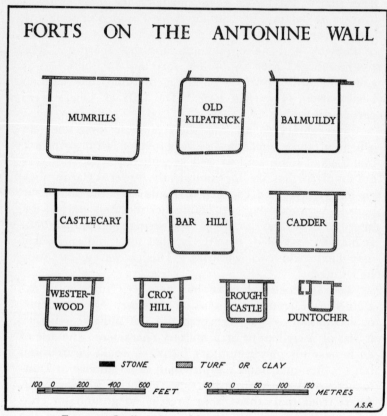

FIG. 19. Outline plans of forts on the Antonine Wall

Antonine Wall forts which have been excavated varied greatly in size, ranging in internal area from Mumrills (6½ acres) to Rough Castle (1 acre) and Duntocher (½ acre) (Fig. 19). Only five or six of them could have held whole cohorts of auxiliary troops.   Mumrills (6½ acres) could have held a milliary cohort.   Old Kilpatrick (4⅙ acres), Balmuildy

(4 acres), Castlecary ($3\frac{1}{2}$ acres), Bar Hill (3 acres) and possibly Cadder ($2\frac{4}{5}$ acres) could have held quingenary cohorts. Old Kilpatrick and Balmuildy may even have held milliary cohorts. The remaining four, Westerwood ($1\frac{9}{10}$ acres), Croy Hill ($1\frac{1}{2}$ acres), Rough Castle (1 acre) and Duntocher ($\frac{1}{2}$ acre) must have had smaller garrisons. It may be that a cohort was subdivided to provide garrisons for two or more forts. It is significant that Castlecary ($3\frac{1}{2}$ acres) was garrisoned for a time by men from a milliary cohort, the First Cohort of Tungri,[1] and that Rough Castle (1 acre) had as its garrison for a time men from the Sixth Cohort of Nervii.[2] On Hadrian's Wall the Sixth Cohort of Nervii occupied a fort, Great Chesters, with an internal area of about 3 acres.[3] It may be noted that an altar erected at Rough Castle to Victory shows that the men from the Sixth Cohort of Nervii who dedicated it were commanded by a centurion of the Twentieth Legion, Flavius Betto.[4] Flavius Betto may have been seconded to command the whole cohort, or perhaps only a part of it.[5]

It was not only in size that the known Antonine Wall forts varied from one another. They differed in their defences and in their shape. Only two, Balmuildy and Castlecary, were girt with a stone wall. The others were defended by ramparts of clay or turf. Four forts only, Balmuildy, Castlecary, Cadder and Rough Castle, were exactly rectangular, the others being rather irregular quadrilaterals. This diversity of the Antonine Wall forts is in sharp contrast to the uniformity of the forts on Hadrian's Wall, and indicates that the two sets of forts were built and garrisoned on an entirely different system.

---

[1] S. N. Miller, *The Roman Fort at Balmuildy* (1922), pp. 108 ff. ; *R.W.*, pp. 412 f.

[2] *R.W.*, pp. 410 ff., 418 f.

[3] *C.I.L.* vii, 726 ; *Handbook to the Roman Wall*, edited by I. A. Richmond (1947), pp. 147 ff.

[4] *R.W.*, pp. 418 f.

[5] Müller, "Abcommandierte Centurionen," in *Philologus*, xli (1882), pp. 482 ff., and v. Domaszewski, *Rangordnung des römischen Heeres*, (1908), pp. 106 f.

The sixteen forts on Hadrian's Wall, spaced at about 5-6 miles apart, were all rectangular (with rounded corners) and were all enclosed by stone walls. Each was garrisoned by a whole cohort or ala of auxiliary troops, many of them derived, it appears, from Wales, and others from the Pennines.[1] The milecastles and turrets on Hadrian's Wall are thought to have been held by patrolling garrisons drawn from some other source than the fort garrisons.[2] From what source, however, and from what units they were drawn, and from whom they received their orders, is not known. The total number of men stationed in milecastles and turrets has been reckoned as about 4000 ; the total number of men stationed in forts on Hadrian's Wall as about 12,000.[3]

The building of the Antonine Wall called into existence not only nineteen forts, closely set at 2-mile intervals, along the Wall itself, but also twenty or more forts and fortlets, strung along a network of roads which covered S. Scotland and apparently penetrated as far north as Perthshire (Fig. 20). Whence came the garrisons for these new Antonine forts and fortlets ?

There is evidence that at the beginning of the Antonine period the milecastles (and presumably the turrets) on Hadrian's Wall were abandoned for a time.[4] Their garrisons then became available for use elsewhere, and, as Mr J. Gillam suggested,[5] they may have been transferred to the fortlets in S. Scotland. The known Antonine fortlets in S. Scotland, however, are fewer than ten in number, and even when all are known they are unlikely to be numerous enough to have absorbed more than a small proportion of the men released from the seventy-nine milecastles on Hadrian's Wall. There would therefore be many, perhaps

---

[1] J. Gillam, in *Trans. Archit. and Arch. Soc. of Durham and Northumberland*, x (1953), p. 361.

[2] *Handbook to the Roman Wall*, edited by I. A. Richmond (1947), p. 28.

[3] *Ibidem.*

[4] *J.R.S.* xl (1950), p. 53.

[5] *Trans. Archit. and Arch. Soc. of Durham and Northumberland*, x (1953), p. 366.

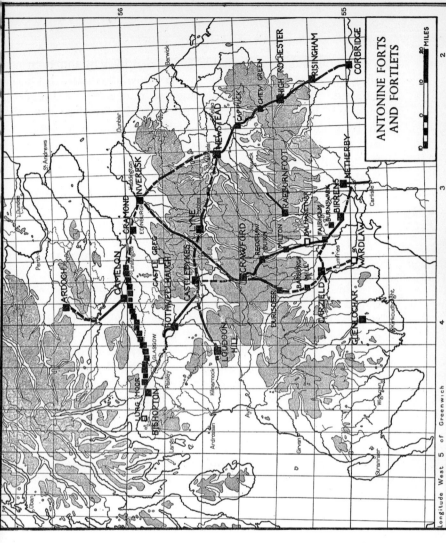

Fig. 20. Map of Antonine Forts and Fortlets in Scotland

Antonine Wall Forts

West to East

Old Kilpatrick
Duntocher
Castlehill
New Kilpatrick
Balmuildy
Cadder
Kirkintilloch
Auchendavy
Bar Hill
Croy Hill
Westerwood
Castlecary
Seabegs
Rough Castle
Falkirk
Mumrills
Inveravon
Kinneil
Bridgeness

a few thousand, men available for service in Scotland even after the Antonine fortlets in the Lowlands had been manned. It is tempting to suggest that some of these men may have been posted to the Antonine Wall to serve in, for example, the " guard-house " between Rough Castle and Falkirk, the small Antonine Wall structures at Wilderness Plantation, east of Balmuildy and at Glasgow Bridge, west of Kirkintilloch, recently discovered from the air by Dr St Joseph, and in very small forts like Westerwood, Croy Hill and Rough Castle (if these were not held by detachments from auxiliary units) or the fortlet and the fort at Duntocher. The presence of such troops at Duntocher might account for the resemblance between the Duntocher fortlet and a Turf Wall milecastle.

The forts on Hadrian's Wall were not, it seems, abandoned during the early Antonine period but, it has been suggested by Mr Gillam[1] and Miss Brenda Swinbank,[2] on the evidence of inscriptions, may have been held by caretaker garrisons of legionary troops. Even if there were not proof of the replacement of auxiliaries by legionaries for this purpose, it would still be reasonable to suppose that when the Antonine Wall was built, part if not all of the auxiliary garrison force on Hadrian's Wall could be released for garrison duty further north.

At least one, and possibly a second, auxiliary unit stationed on Hadrian's Wall in the reign of Hadrian has also left epigraphic evidence of its presence on the Antonine Wall. The First Cohort of Hamii was at Carvoran in A.D. 136-138,[3] and was subsequently on the Antonine Wall at Bar Hill,[4] whence it returned to Carvoran about A.D. 163 in the governorship of Calpurnius Agricola.[3] The First Cohort of Tungri was possibly at Birdoswald under Hadrian.[5]

---

[1] *Trans. Archit. and Arch. Soc. of Durham and Northumberland*, x (1953), pp. 368 f.

[2] *Ibidem*, pp. 391 ff.

[3] *C.I.L.* vii, 748 ; *Proc. Soc. Ant. Newcastle* (4), ix (1939-42), p. 250 ; *Handbook to the Roman Wall*, edited by I. A. Richmond (1947), p. 157 ; E. Birley, *The Centenary Pilgrimage of Hadrian's Wall* (1949), p. 62.

[4] *R.W.*, pp. 425 f.   [5] E. Birley, in *Germania*, xxiii (1939), pp. 189 f.

It was certainly stationed for a time at Castlecary on the Antonine Wall,[1] and from Severus onwards held the fort at Housesteads on Hadrian's Wall.[2]

There are two other auxiliary units which served both on Hadrian's Wall and on the Antonine Wall, but contrary to Mr Gillam's view,[3] they were not certainly present on Hadrian's Wall in the reign of Hadrian himself. One of these, the Fourth Cohort of Gauls, set up an altar at Castlehill, on the Antonine Wall,[4] a building inscription at Risingham, on the eastern route into Scotland,[5] and altars at Castlesteads on Hadrian's Wall,[6] and several inscriptions at Chesterholm.[7] It was not until the early third century that the Fourth Cohort of Gauls reached Chesterholm,[8] and Mr Eric Birley has informed me that he believes that the Castlesteads altars seem to go best into the closing years of the second century, and that the sculptured setting of the Risingham inscription seems to fit the time of Lollius Urbicus. In that case, the Cohort must have come north to Castlehill from Risingham, during but possibly not at the beginning of the Antonine period.

The other auxiliary unit, the Sixth Cohort of Nervii, was at Rough Castle on the Antonine Wall,[9] and was also at Great Chesters on Hadrian's Wall, at an unknown date.[10] The altar which it set up at Great Chesters seems to Mr Birley, by the style of the lettering, easier to assign to the time of Commodus than to that of Hadrian.

---

[1] *R.W.*, pp. 412 f.

[2] *C.I.L.* vii, 633, 635, 638 etc. ; *Handbook to the Roman Wall*, edited by I. A. Richmond (1947), pp. 112 ff. ; E. Birley, *The Centenary Pilgrimage of Hadrian's Wall* (1949), p. 47.

[3] *Trans. Archit. and Arch. Soc. of Durham and Northumberland*, x (1953), p. 368.   [4] *R.W.*, pp. 433 f.

[5] *C.I.L.* vii, 1001.   [6] *C.I.L.* vii, 877 f.

[7] *C.I.L.* vii, 703 f., 715 ; *Handbook to the Roman Wall*, edited by I. A. Richmond (1947), p. 136.

[8] *Ibidem* ; E. Birley, *The Centenary Pilgrimage of Hadrian's Wall* (1949), p. 54.

[9] *R.W.*, p. 411 and pp. 418 f.

[10] *C.I.L.* vii, 269 ; *Handbook to the Roman Wall*, edited by I. A. Richmond (1947), p. 147.

Even, however, if there were evidence that the entire
auxiliary force on Hadrian's Wall was sent north when the
Antonine Wall was built, it would not have sufficed to
provide garrisons for even all the known Antonine forts in
Scotland. Garrisons would have had to be sought from
sources other than Hadrian's Wall.

One such source was apparently the north of England
between Derby and the Tyne. Several forts in that area
(with the exception of those on the Cumberland coast)
seem to have been deprived of their garrisons in the early
Antonine period.[1]

Another source of supply for Antonine Wall garrisons,
it was long ago suggested by Sir George Macdonald,[2]
may have been the legionary force in Britain, contrary though
it was to normal Roman practice to use legionary troops
as frontier garrisons. Certainly inscriptions show that
legionaries built several of the Antonine Wall forts, that
legionaries were buried in the cemetery beside the fort at
Auchendavy, and that legionaries dedicated altars to their
favourite deities while operating in some capacity on the
Antonine Wall.

There is definite proof too that at least one of the forts
in S. Scotland, the most important fort on the eastern
route, at Newstead on the Tweed, had for a time a detach-
ment of the Twentieth Legion as part of its garrison.[3]
A hint that Newstead may not have been the only S. Scottish
fort with legionaries in its garrison force was recently provided by the discovery of a stone carved with one of the
emblems of the Second Legion, a capricorn, during
the excavation of the Antonine fort at Castledykes, on the
Clyde. Men of the Second Legion must have been present
at Castledykes, but whether as builders of the fort or as
part of its garrison, is, however, not certain.[4]

Still, the evidence from Newstead shows that legionaries

[1] *Trans. Archit. and Arch. Soc. of Durham and Northumberland*, x (1953), pp.
362 and 398.
[2] *R.W.*, pp. 439 ff.
[3] *P.S.A.S.* LXXXIV (1950), pp. 21 ff.   [4] *J.R.S.* XLI (1951), p. 120.

were used to eke out the garrison force needed in S. Scotland. There is, then, no longer any justification for rejecting out of hand, as has sometimes been done,[1] the possibility that legionaries also served as garrison troops on the Antonine Wall itself. Proof may still be absent, but not possibility or even probability.

Whatever the character and source of the garrison force sent north to hold the Antonine forts and fortlets in Scotland, it is likely that economies would have to be effected in the use of it, where this could be done with safety. One such economy may have been the association of small forts with large forts on the Antonine Wall. If so, there was no doubt some reason for the placing of small, instead of large, forts at certain points, although our knowledge of the Antonine Wall forts in general is as yet too incomplete to justify an attempt to determine the reason. There is not, for example, evidence that small forts alternated with large forts or that small forts, like those at Rough Castle, Westerwood, Croy Hill and Duntocher, were placed on sites particularly strong by nature. The sites of almost all Antonine Wall forts were strong by nature.

Some time after it was first built, the Antonine fort at Duntocher, and its military enclosure, underwent repair and modification of plan. The north rampart of the fort had an extension built on to its south side, either to increase the width of the rampart, or to serve as a sentry path. The stone base of the extension included at least one squared building stone, perhaps from a ruined building. Roads through the west and north fort gateways at least, and the *intervallum* street behind the north rampart, were also wholly or partly relaid.

The small squarish building in the centre of the fort went out of use, possibly after being destroyed, and over its foundations were laid the foundations of a long narrow building. The southern part of the latter stood over a

---

[1] *E.g.* by Miss B. Swinbank, in *Trans. Archit. and Arch. Soc. of Durham and Northumberland*, x (1953), p. 385.

considerable depth of made-up soil containing occupation debris. The long building, like its predecessor, may have served the purpose of an administrative building.

A new series of post-holes east of the long building, with their stone packing still intact, indicates that here, if not elsewhere in the fort, wooden structures, probably barrack blocks, had been repaired or even rebuilt. In the military enclosure too, early post-holes cut into the subsoil were covered over by cobbling (as was indeed all or most of the whole internal area of the enclosure), and were replaced by other post-holes dug down through forced soil. Their stone packing too was intact, and as with the early post-holes in the enclosure they seem to have belonged to two wooden buildings, possibly barracks, separated by a central road. The westerly building at least lay very close to the rampart, but this rampart was of course no longer an outer rampart of an isolated structure. The cobbling in the enclosure also continued south to cover fallen turf lying over the large post-holes of its south gate. The original massive gate structure was probably replaced at this time by a gate of more modest proportions. If so, the original massive north gate may have been replaced by a smaller gate at this time too, rather than when the fort was first built. Finally, in the north-east sector of the fort, an oven seems to have been either repaired or else built anew.

The other Antonine Wall forts which have been extensively excavated within recent years, for example at Mumrills,[1] Rough Castle,[2] Cadder,[3] Balmuildy[4] and Old Kilpatrick,[5] have provided evidence for thoroughgoing repair and even reconstruction on at least two occasions before they were finally abandoned. There were thus three periods of occupation on the Antonine Wall itself,[6] and

---

[1] *P.S.A.S.* LXIII (1929), p. 574.

[2] *P.S.A.S.* LXVII (1933), pp. 243 ff. ; *R.W.*, pp. 219 ff.

[3] John Clarke, *The Roman Fort at Cadder* (1933), pp. 87 ff.

[4] S. N. Miller, *The Roman Fort at Balmuildy* (1922), pp. 104 ff.

[5] S. N. Miller, *The Roman Fort at Old Kilpatrick* (1928), pp. 57 f. ; *P.S.A.S.* LXVI (1932), pp. 220 ff.   [6] *R.W.*, pp. 477 ff.

apparently also at the fort at Whitemoss, Bishopton, on the south bank of the Clyde.[1] Only two Antonine periods, however, have been identified in the excavated forts in S. Scotland which are not on the Antonine Wall, for example, at Newstead,[2] Cappuck[3] and Castledykes.[4] Of the known Antonine forts north of the Wall, none has been excavated recently and extensively enough to warrant a statement about the number of its Antonine occupations.

At Duntocher only two Antonine periods have been identified with certainty (subsequent at least to the completion of the Antonine Wall), unless the close juxtaposition of pairs of stone-packed post-holes in the military enclosure is evidence of a third. No other such evidence was noted, either because the remains were too hopelessly disturbed for it to have survived, or else because it never existed. If the latter, then Duntocher, like the Antonine forts in S. Scotland not on the Wall itself, played no part in the third Antonine Wall period, whatever the date of that period was.

Sir George Macdonald's view on the three Antonine Wall periods, and on the date at which the Wall was finally abandoned are well known. He held that the Antonine Wall forts (so far excavated) had been twice damaged or destroyed by enemy attacks, and had been twice reoccupied and repaired by the Romans.[5] The probable dates of the two destructions and reoccupations, he suggested, were about A.D. 155 and A.D. 184.

The evidence for the date of the first destruction and reoccupation is provided by coins of A.D. 155 commemorating a Roman victory in Britain, by an inscription set up at Newcastle during the governorship of Julius Verus by reinforcements sent from Germany to Britain to fill gaps in the ranks of the three legions stationed in Britain, and by the

---

[1] *J.R.S.*, XLIII (1953), pp. 105 f., and XLV (1955), p. 123.
[2] *P.S.A.S.* LXXXIV (1950), pp. 11 ff.
[3] *P.S.A.S.* LXXXV (1951), pp. 139 ff.
[4] *The Roman Occupation of South-Western Scotlaed* (1952), pp. 169 ff.
[5] *R.W.*, pp. 477 ff.

H

building or rebuilding of certain forts in the north, for example at Birrens, Dumfriesshire, at Netherby, Cumberland, and at Brough in Derbyshire, also during the governorship of Julius Verus. His term of office seems to have begun about A.D. 157.[1] The Birrens inscription is dated to A.D. 158. Sir George Macdonald suggested that the coins, dated A.D. 155, commemorated the initial success of the Roman reoccupation, while the building or rebuilding of forts, and the reinforcement of the British army, marked the final stage.

The evidence for the second abandonment and reoccupation of the Antonine Wall is derived from coins of Commodus dated to A.D. 184, 185 and 186,[2] commemorating once again a Roman victory in Britain, and from the *Historia Augusta*[3] and Dio Cassius.[4] The *Historia Augusta* records a revolt in Britain, and Dio Cassius states that " the tribes in the island having crossed the wall that separated them from the cantonments of the Romans, wrought great havoc, and slew a Roman general with the soldiers under his command. Commodus thereupon in great alarm sent Ulpius Marcellus against them. . . . Marcellus inflicted terrible punishment on the barbarians in Britain." Sir George Macdonald believed that the Antonine Wall was reoccupied after Marcellus' punitive expedition, but that it was abandoned shortly afterwards.[5]

Sir George's suggested dating has been provisionally accepted by many scholars, sometimes with slight reservations. Mr Clarke, for example, found evidence at Cadder that the third period was marked by " an occupation in force, for which some permanence was anticipated, certainly before evacuation was an immediate prospect.

---

[1] Haverfield, in *P.S.A.S.* xxxviii (1904), pp. 454 ff. ; and *R.W.*, pp. 10 f.

[2] The latest of these coins are assigned to December, A.D. 185, by Mattingly and Sydenham, *Roman Imperial Coinage*, iii (1930), p. 419, No. 459e, and in *Coins of the Roman Empire in the British Museum*, iv (1940), p. 802, rather than to A.D. 186.

[3] *Vit. Comm. Ant.*, 13, 5 and 8, 4.

[4] Dio Cassius, lxxii, 8.   [5] *R.W.*, p. 479.

Under these circumstances the most probable date for the beginning of the third occupation is shortly after A.D. 170, following the trouble which we are told was threatening in Britain in A.D. 169." [1]

Mr S. N. Miller, too, found that the results of his own excavations at Balmuildy [2] and at Old Kilpatrick [3] were in general agreement with Sir George Macdonald's interpretation of the history of the Wall. He also, however, like Mr Clarke, thought that the second disaster might have taken place as early as about A.D. 170, rather than about A.D. 180, even although at Balmuildy " some of the reconstructive work gave the impression of being a mere temporary makeshift, like the work of men who already anticipated an early evacuation," [4] and at Old Kilpatrick the perfunctory rebuilding suggested that the " second disaster may have been ' a mere episode of the final abandonment.' " [5]

A well-known passage in Pausanias recording a Brigantian raid in the reign of Antoninus Pius into the Genounian district which is subject to Rome [6] (a district otherwise unknown), has also been the subject of a most penetrating discussion by Mr Miller in an attempt to elucidate events in Scotland during the Antonine period. Sir George Macdonald had himself inclined to the view that the Brigantian raid may have been connected with the disturbances of about A.D. 155. [7] Mr Miller has recently suggested that the Antonine Wall garrisons may have been deliberately withdrawn about this time to deal with a Brigantian rising in their rear, thus exposing the forts in Scotland to enemy violence. [8] Mr Eric Birley has, on the

---

[1] *Vit. M. Ant. Phil.*, 22, 1 ; cf. *ibidem*, 8, 7 and *R.W.*, p. 11 ; John Clarke, *The Roman Fort at Cadder* (1933), p. 89.

[2] S. N. Miller, *The Roman Fort at Balmuildy* (1922), pp. 104 ff.

[3] S. N. Miller, *The Roman Fort at Old Kilpatrick* (1928), pp. 57 f.

[4] S. N. Miller, *The Roman Fort at Balmuildy* (1922), pp. 104 f.

[5] S. N. Miller, *The Roman Fort at Old Kilpatrick* (1928), p. 58.

[6] *Descript. Græc.*, VIII, 43, 4.

[7] *R.W.*, pp. 10 f.

[8] *The Roman Occupation of South-Western Scotland* (1952), pp. 222 ff.

other hand, summarised arguments for the belief that the passage in Pausanias refers to the events of A.D. 142 which preceded the building of the Antonine Wall.[1]

Latterly, too, Mr Miller abandoned Sir George Macdonald's view of the date at which the Antonine Wall was evacuated, in favour of a theory that the Wall may have been reoccupied for a brief time by Severus in A.D. 210, and that the puzzling third period found on the Antonine Wall alone and absent from other Antonine forts in Scotland may belong to that date.[2] It has to be admitted, however, that no matter how interesting and attractive may be such an explanation of the third period on the Antonine Wall, the Antonine Wall forts have not so far provided the least scrap of dated evidence for a Severan occupation.

Still more recently, Mr J. P. Gillam has challenged Sir George Macdonald's dating of the three Antonine Wall periods, on the grounds that there is evidence for increased activity to the south of, and on the line of, Hadrian's Wall, including the reoccupation of milecastles and turrets, in about A.D. 163, during the governorship of Calpurnius Agricola.[3] The Antonine Wall, Mr Gillam has argued, could not have been occupied in strength contemporaneously with Hadrian's Wall, and must therefore have been evacuated for a period of some years after A.D. 163. In support of this argument, he has pointed to the apparent absence of dated inscriptions and of closely datable pottery (stamped Samian ware and mortaria) of the period beginning early in the sixties from the Antonine Wall, but not from Newstead. (It may be said at this juncture that a careful study at first hand of the pottery from Newstead and that from the Antonine Wall forts indicates that, in general, it is all of the same character.)

---

[1] *Trans. Dumfriesshire and Galloway Nat. Hist. and Ant. Soc.*, XXIX (1952), pp. 46 ff.

[2] *Cambridge Ancient History*, XII (1939), p. 40, and *The Roman Occupation of South-Western Scotland* (1952), pp. 235 ff.

[3] *Trans. Archit. and Arch. Soc. of Durham and Northumberland*, X (1953), pp. 359 ff.

Mr Gillam has suggested, too, that distance slabs and altars from the Antonine Wall were buried in an orderly evacuation which took place in the early sixties, and not, as usually supposed, when the Antonine Wall was finally abandoned. The truth is that there is little, if any, real evidence that any of the distance slabs or altars from the Antonine Wall were ever at any time " carefully buried to preserve them from desecration."

Mr Gillam's tentative dating of the Antonine Wall periods is as follows : " Period I certainly began in A.D. 142, and we may suggest that it ended in A.D. 163, when Calpurnius Agricola withdrew the frontier southwards because of threatened outbreaks behind the lines. Period II may have begun in A.D. 184, when war had become an alarming reality and Commodus realised, as Antoninus Pius had realised before him, that the main threat was from a combination of tribes beyond the reach of the provincial army. This period ended, we may be sure, in the general destruction of A.D. 197, and not in an immediate evacuation. Period III may then be ascribed, with Miller and Birley, to the third century." [1]

This interpretation, as Mr Gillam himself is the first to point out, is open to objections. The principal objections are " that no late second- or third-century coins have been found on the Antonine Wall, and that the description of the invasion in A.D. 181 seems to imply that the Wall that the tribes crossed was occupied by troops." [1]

The Antonine Wall itself has not yet, unfortunately, provided decisive evidence for the dating of its three periods. There is a dearth of dated inscriptions from it, and an almost complete lack of stratified coin finds. Even stratified pottery has seldom been recorded from Antonine Wall forts, and pottery is, in any case, not a completely reliable guide when a close dating is sought.

At Duntocher, a careful watch was kept for stratified material from below the secondary buildings and roads

---

[1] *Trans. Archit. and Arch. Soc. of Durham and Northumberland*, x (1953), p. 375.

which might help to date the end of the first Antonine occupation of the fort. Practically none was recovered, however, doubtless owing to the ruthless destruction to which the remains had been subjected in recent times. There were only a fragment of the base of a mortarium of hard white clay, and a fragment of the rim of a coarse fumed bowl found under the cobbling of the road through the north gate of the fort, and an olla base of coarse fumed ware found below the cobbling inside the south gate of the military enclosure. (The fragment of a grey olla and the base of another from the top of the easterly narrow trench in the enclosure may be added even although the trenches may have dated only to the occupation of the fortlet as an independent structure and have been filled before the first Antonine occupation of the fort and military enclosure.)

These potsherds may be of interest as being among the very few stratified potsherds so far recorded from the Antonine Wall. The coarse fumed ware, in particular, seems to fit suitably into the early part of the Antonine occupation. They cannot, however, provide a *terminus post quem* for the end of the first Antonine occupation as unequivocally dated coins would have done.

The occupation of Duntocher, and of other Antonine forts in Scotland, continued at least until fine fumed ware and large Samian platters of the form 31 R were in use, and apparently until coins of Commodus were reaching Scotland. The latest coin from the Antonine Wall which has been certainly identified is an *as* of Marcus Aurelius, of A.D. 173-174, found in 1952 at Mumrills. A coin (or coins) of Commodus, which must have been minted in or after A.D. 175 are reported from Kirkintilloch, and a much worn brass coin from Bar Hill has been identified by Sir George Macdonald as "Commodus (possible)." [1] The latest coin found on an Antonine fort in Scotland, which is not on the Antonine Wall, is a *denarius* of Crispina,

[1] *P.S.A.S.* LII (1918), pp. 223 f.

wife of Commodus, from Newstead.[1] Crispina married Commodus in A.D. 178, and coins bearing her name may have been issued as early as that date, although she and Commodus did not become emperor and empress until the death of Marcus Aurelius in A.D. 180.[2] The Antonine system in Scotland was therefore in existence until at least A.D. 178.

The recent discovery of a hoard of Roman silver coins at Briglands, near Rumbling Bridge, Kinross-shire, almost certainly carries its life down to at least A.D. 186. In all, 170 *denarii* were found at Briglands, ranging in date from the emperors Nero to Commodus. There were seven coins of Commodus, as emperor, and of these, one was of A.D. 180,[3] one of A.D. 181, two of A.D. 181-182, one of A.D. 183, one of A.D. 183-184, and one of A.D. 186-187. The chronological sequence of these seven coins suggests that the owner of the hoard was adding steadily to his savings up to the year A.D. 186 at least, and was including newly minted coins of each year as they came his way. There must then have been some source open to him, from which he could acquire newly minted coins, up to at least the year A.D. 186. The source can hardly have been any other than the Antonine garrison force in Scotland. If so, the Antonine system in Scotland must have remained in existence until at least A.D. 186.[4] The reason why the latest coin from the Briglands hoard is later than the latest coin from an Antonine fort in Scotland, is due to the fact that coins in a hoard were deliberately and regularly withdrawn from circulation by its owner, while coins from a site find were dropped or lost accidentally and involuntarily, probably with long intervals between each loss.

[1] J. Curle, *The Fort of Newstead* (1911), p. 399.

[2] *Coins of the Roman Empire in the British Museum*, IV (1940), pp. cxiii, cliv, 693 ff.

[3] The coin of A.D. 180 is assigned by Mattingly and Sydenham, *Roman Imperial Coinage*, III (1930), p. 366, no. 2, to the beginning of Commodus' own reign, but in *Coins of the Roman Empire in the British Museum*, IV (1940), p. 508, no. 811, is placed at the very end of the reign of Marcus Aurelius.

[4] *P.S.A.S.* LXXXIV (1950), pp. 149 f.

The good condition of the latest coins in the Briglands hoard suggests that they had not been long in circulation before the date of concealment, so that a date in or shortly after A.D. 186-187 for the burial and loss of the hoard seems a probable one. Indeed, the loss of the hoard may well have been caused by the unsettled conditions which arose in North Britain in the reign of Commodus, apparently as a result of a revolt by tribes north of the Antonine Wall.[1] Coins of Commodus dating to A.D. 184 and 185, if not to A.D. 186,[2] and commemorating victories in Britain, indicate that the rising of the North Britons took some considerable time to put down. Even if the Antonine system continued in operation until A.D. 186 or later, and Roman coins still passed from Roman into other hands, the life and property of even the most peace-loving North Briton north of the Antonine Wall may well have been insecure.

Pending the discovery of stratified datable evidence for the history of the Antonine period in Scotland, it may be accepted with certainty that the Antonine Wall and Antonine system of roads, forts and fortlets were established in about A.D. 142, and were still in use in the early part of Commodus' reign, probably until at least A.D. 186. If they remained in existence later than that, they cannot have survived the destruction of Hadrian's Wall by the northern barbarians in A.D. 196 or 197, when the usurper Albinus took the army of Britain over to Gaul to fight against the emperor Severus.[3] Since Hadrian's Wall was destroyed at that time, the Antonine system, if still in existence, must have been wiped out too.

During the Antonine period, the Antonine Wall forts (except possibly Duntocher) and the fort at Bishopton were twice damaged or destroyed and twice repaired or reconstructed. The first destruction may have taken place either about A.D. 155 or about A.D. 163. The second may

---

[1] See above, p. 114.   [2] See above, p. 114 n.
[3] Dio Cassius, LXXVI, 6, 2 ; S. N. Miller, in *Cambridge Ancient History*, XII (1939), pp. 36 ff.

have taken place either about A.D. 170 or about A.D. 184. There is no evidence from the Antonine Wall itself to indicate how long or how short were the intervals between the three occupations. All that is certain is that reoccupation of the forts followed each of the two destructions after an interval long enough for a decision to be taken to change the garrisons in some, but not in all, of the forts,[1] and to make certain modifications in some, but not in all, of the fort-plans, but not long enough for the forts to become so derelict that they could not be occupied as they stood.

The other Antonine forts in S. Scotland have so far yielded evidence for only one destruction and one rebuilding. At Newstead, at least, the second occupation seems to have followed closely on the first.[2] The reason why there were two, instead of three, occupations of the Antonine forts in S. Scotland may be the simple, if not entirely convincing, one that they escaped the second destruction which befell the forts on the Antonine Wall itself.[3] The future excavation of Antonine forts north of the Forth-Clyde line should, by determining how many periods of occupation they had, throw light on the significance of the three Antonine Wall periods, and the two Antonine periods in forts in S. Scotland. And a deliberate search for stratified finds in an Antonine Wall fort less sadly battered than the fort at Duntocher may yet recover evidence for the dates of the three Antonine Wall periods.[4]

[1] *R.W.*, pp. 440 f.

[2] *P.S.A.S.* LXXXIV (1950), p. 14.

[3] *The Roman Occupation of South-Western Scotland* (1952), p. 234.

[4] Rough Castle, for example, with its two additional rampart bases, and its two additional (east) annexe ramparts, may be suspected of still suppressing stratified evidence.

APPENDIX I

Report on Material containing Iron Pipe [1]

By J. A. SMYTHE, PH.D., D.SC., Newcastle-on-Tyne

A LARGE mass weighing 2 lb. 14 oz., in shape like a stalactite, 7 in. long, 3 in. by 2½ in. at top and 2 in. diameter at bottom. This is made up of concretionary white mineral, rather like magnesium limestone in appearance and consisting mostly of carbonate. Though holey it has considerable strength and a large rounded pebble of fine-grained micaceous sandstone from the surrounding earth was firmly cemented to the mass of carbonate. The whole material is glazed with a thin film of translucent matter. A 1 in. pipe passes vertically through the mass. It is blocked completely over two-thirds of its length, partly over the remaining (top) third, with the carbonate which forms the main bulk of the specimen.

The chemical examination of the object is described under three headings, viz. :

1. The main mass of carbonate, external to the pipe and partly filling it.
2. The pipe.
3. The glaze.

1. *The main mass.* On extraction with water this yields ·75 per cent. of soluble matter, alkaline in reaction, consisting of ammonium carbonate, along with some nitrate. Chloride is absent. The residue from the extraction, dried at 110° C., gave an analysis :

Sol. in dil. HCl	$\begin{cases} H_2O \\ CO_2 \\ MgO \end{cases}$	$\begin{matrix} 16\cdot0 \\ 22\cdot8 \\ 50\cdot9 \end{matrix}$	Proved absent were sulphur and calcium. A little phosphate is present.
Insol. in dil. HCl	$\begin{cases} SiO_2 \\ Al_2O_3 + H_2O_3 \end{cases}$	$\begin{matrix} 4\cdot3 \\ 5\cdot9 \end{matrix}$	The insoluble part contains some grit and clayey matter.

99·9

---

[1] See above, p. 50.

The first three constituents in this list are in combination in the form of basic carbonate of magnesium, and this makes up 89·7 per cent of the whole. Calculated to 100 per cent. the proportions of the three constituents are :

H_2O	17·9
CO_2	25·4
MgO	56·7
	100·0

2. *The pipe.* When freed from adhering carbonate, the pipe is dark grey in colour and both outside and inside surfaces are free from pitting. It is extremely hard and after crushing it yielded to the magnet 8 per cent. of its weight of metallic iron. It yielded on analysis (after removal of the metal) :

H_2O	2·2
CO_2	2·1
MgO	23·8
SiO_2	4·1
Al_2O_3	60·9
ZiO	7·4
	100·5

The H_2O and CO_2 and an amount of MgO equivalent to the CO_2 (2 per cent.) may be taken to be present as adhering carbonate (total 6·4 per cent.). The amount of MgO not allocated in this way is 23·8 — 2·0 = 21·8 per cent. One may assume that, say, 4 per cent. of Al_2O_3 is taken up by combination with the silica (not present as sand) in clay-like form, leaving 60·9 — 4·0 = 56·9 per cent. of Al_2O_3 unallocated.

Most of the iron returned in the analysis as ferrous oxide is probably present as metallic iron which has escaped removal by the magnetic treatment.

The problem, then, is to determine the mode of combination of the 21·8 per cent. magnesia and the 56·9 per cent. of alumina, and, chemically speaking, the only likelihood is as an aluminate of magnesia, $MgOAl_2O_3$, which is the formula of the mineral spinel. As the molecular ratio of the two quantities is almost 1 : 1, this seems the likely explanation. A better method of illustrating the relationship is to compare the composition, calculated to 100 per cent., with that of pure spinel.

	Material from pipe	Spinel
MgO	27·7	28·4
Al_2O_3	72·3	71·6
	100·0	100·0

This inference is supported by the excessive hardness of the pipe, for spinel has the hardness 8, on Moh's scale (corundum is 9 and diamond is 10 on this scale).

3. *The glaze.* This is exceedingly thin, but tough, so that small quantities can be peeled off where the surface covered with it is smooth, as in the case of the sandstone pebble. It was isolated in larger quantity, by dissolving the carbonate from a sample of the main mass in warm, diluted hydrochloric acid, which liberated patches of the glaze within the inside of the specimen.

This glaze is of organic origin ; it is soluble in acetone and the filtered solution, on evaporation of the solvent, leaves a snow-white residue. When touched with a small flame, the glaze flashes like gunpowder. On dry distillation it is carbonised and brown fumes of oxides of nitrogen are evolved, and it is carbonised by warming with concentrated sulphuric acid. It is apparently an explosive of the nitro-compound group, like lyddite, trinitrotoluene, or nitro-cellulose.

So far as the immediate object of this examination is concerned, it is evident that this object is not of Roman origin. The iron pipe alone would be sufficient proof of this. It may be added that there is no trace of lead present, or of such metals as copper and tin, commonly found in Roman remains. The sequence of events leading to the formation of the object may be something like this :

An iron pipe was used to discharge the effluent (presumably from a chemical works) rich in aluminium and magnesium compounds (the latter presumably as the soluble bicarbonate). The basic carbonate of magnesium was rapidly precipitated, owing to loss of carbon dioxide, and this blocked the pipe, so that the liquor flooded over the outside and built up the main mass of stalactitic carbonate. Meanwhile the iron of the pipe was replaced in great part by magnesium aluminate, or similar spinel-like compound. At the end of this discharge, a solution of some explosive compound, presumably in some organic solvent like acetone, was passed through, and from this was deposited the material of the glaze.

APPENDIX II

THROUGH the kindness of Mr Charles Taylor, Dr J. F. Hyslop, of the analytical staff of Messrs John G. Stein & Co., Ltd., of Castlecary, analysed three pieces of brick or tile which appeared not to be Roman.[1] Mr Taylor adds to Dr Hyslop's analysis the note that " our opinion is that the material has been obtained in the vicinity of Duntocher as there are large deposits of similar marl on the Kilsyth Hills, especially in Corrie Glen." This view, and the analyses, suggest that the three pieces of brick or tile did not come from a Roman tileworks.

Analyses of three samples of bricks or tiles, from Duntocher

By Dr J. F. HYSLOP

	1. Per cent.	2. Per cent.	3. Per cent.
SiO_2 (Silica)	58·29	58·96	41·51
Al_2O_3 (Aluminium Oxide)	25·70	28·39	26·82
Fe_2O_3 (Iron Oxide)	13·04	10·13	25·92
TiO_2 (Titanium Oxide)	1·48	1·30	1·92
MgO (Magnesium Oxide)	0·42	0·44	0·91
CaO (Calcium Oxide)	traces	traces	1·42
Na_2O (Sodium Oxide)	0·32	0·38	0·34
K_2O (Potassium Oxide)	0·82	0·70	0·48
	100·17	100.30	99·32
Loss over 109° C.	0·59	0·74	21·89
Carbon			2·02

These analyses are unusual for ceramic ware. The first point to note is the high alumina +iron oxide content, and the second is the absence of the usual fluxes, magnesia, lime, soda and potash.

[1] See above, pp. 52, 59, 73.

The composition is the same type as the Campsie Corrie Glen marl, a typical analysis of which is :

	Per cent.
SiO_2	53·86
Al_2O_3	27·36
Fe_2O_3	12·48
TiO_2	2·80
MgO	1·37
CaO	1·96
Na_2O	0·12
K_2O	0·60

INDEX

I

PRINTED IN GREAT BRITAIN BY
OLIVER AND BOYD LTD.
EDINBURGH